0816138

CW01292373

SPINOZA'S *ETHICS*

Continuum Reader's Guides

Aristotle's Nicomachean Ethics – Christopher Warne

Hegel's Philosophy of Right – David Rose

Heidegger's Being and Time – William Blattner

Hobbes's Leviathan – Laurie Bagby

Hume's Dialogues Concerning Natural Religion – Andrew Pyle

Hume's Enquiry Concerning Human Understanding – Alan Bailey and Dan O'Brian

Kant's Critique of Pure Reason – James Luchte

Locke's Essay Concerning Human Understanding – William Uzgalis

Mill's On Liberty – Geoffrey Scarre

Nietzsche's On the Genealogy of Morals – Daniel Conway

Plato's Republic – Luke Purshouse

Wittgenstein's Tractatus Logico Philosophicus – Roger M. White

SPINOZA'S *ETHICS*
A Reader's Guide

J. THOMAS COOK

continuum

Continuum
The Tower Building   80 Maiden Lane, Suite 704
11 York Road   New York
London SE1 7NX   NY 10038

www.continuumbooks.com

© J. Thomas Cook 2007

All rights reserved. No part of this publication may be reproduced or transmitted in any form or by any means, electronic or mechanical, including photocopying, recording, or any information storage or retrieval system, without prior permission in writing from the publishers.

J. Thomas Cook has asserted his right under the Copyright, Designs and Patents Act, 1988, to be identified as Author of this work.

British Library Cataloguing-in-Publication Data
A catalogue record for this book is available from the British Library.

ISBN: 0-8264-8915-X (hardback)
978-08264-8915-9
0-8264-8916-8 (paperback)
978-08264-8916-6

Library of Congress Cataloging-in-Publication Data
Cook, J. Thomas.
  Spinoza's ethics: a reader's guide / J. Thomas Cook.
  p. cm.
  Includes bibliograpical references.
  ISBN-13: 978-0-8264-8915-9 (hardback)
  ISBN-10: 0-8264-8915-X (hardback)
  ISBN-13: 978-0-8264-8916-6 (pbk.)
  ISBN-10: 0-8264-8916-8 (pbk.)
  1. Spinoza, Benedictus de, 1632–1677. Ethica. 2. Ethics. I. Title.

B3974.C66 2007
170–dc22
                                                    2007011407

Typeset by YHT Ltd, London
Printed and bound in Great Britain by
MPG Books Ltd, Bodmin, Cornwall

CONTENTS

Acknowledgements	vii
Preface	viii
1. Spinoza and the *Ethics*: background and context	1
2. Main themes and influences	8
3. Reading the text	15
Part 1 – On God	
Part 2 – On the Nature and Origin of the Mind	
Part 3 – On the Origin and Nature of the Affects	
Part 4 – Of Human Bondage, or the Power of the Emotions	
Part 5 – On the Power of the Intellect, or On Human Freedom	
4. The influence of the *Ethics*	151
Notes for further reading	163
Index	167

For

Patricia

with love and gratitude

ACKNOWLEDGEMENTS

I have been reading and thinking about Spinoza's *Ethics* since I first encountered the text in an undergraduate lecture course with Maurice Mandelbaum in the 1970s. My interest was subsequently further piqued and developed in classes and conversations with John Lachs over a period of 5 years. Amelie O. Rorty and Ed Curley, in their NEH Summer Seminars (and ongoing conversations since then), have been extremely valuable in developing my understanding. Over the years I have learned from and been challenged by colleagues, friends and students – too many to name – at a number of institutions, conferences and seminars in the US as well as in Europe and Israel. Sincere thanks to all of these.

The members of the Department of Philosophy and Religion at Rollins College have provided a supportive atmosphere over the years, and I am grateful for their help and for their tolerance of my rather obsessive focus on Spinoza. I am also happy to acknowledge the help of the participants in my 2006 senior seminar on the *Ethics* who read through much of Chapter 3 of the manuscript of this *Guide* and provided valuable suggestions and feedback.

Thanks to Knowledge Products, Inc., of Nashville, Tennessee, for their kind permission to use material that first appeared in the script for the Spinoza segment of the Giants of Philosophy audiotape series.

Special thanks, too, to Karen Lane, for her generous help with the book's index.

Finally, I gratefully acknowledge the excellent support and encouragement from the editorial staff at Continuum Press for keeping the project in motion and on target.

PREFACE

Spinoza's *Ethics* is univerally recognized as a masterwork of early modern philosophy. But it also strikes the newcomer as a singularly formidable work. Composed in the 'geometrical manner', and couched in an unfamiliar philosophical vocabulary, it presents a daunting challenge to the first-time reader.

While the form and terminology of the *Ethics* can seem alien, the philosophical system that Spinoza presents in the work is in many ways remarkably modern in its outlook. Proceeding rationally, taking science seriously and regarding human beings from a strictly naturalistic perspective, Spinoza offers a psychological diagnosis of the source of our discontents and proposes a therapeutic program of emotional and ethical self-improvement that leads to freedom, contentment and even blessedness. Along the way he addresses still-current questions about God, purpose, human finitude, illusion and liberation.

The serious student of the history of philosophy will find in Spinoza a pivotal and radical thinker at the dawn of modernity. The general reader today might encounter a kindred spirit and a world-view not so drastically different from our own. This *Reader's Guide* is written in hopes of making the *Ethics* more accessible and more engaging for contemporary readers at all levels.

The first chapter sketches the biographical and historical context that provides the background for the *Ethics*. Chapter 2 outlines and explains four major themes – 'big ideas' – orienting the reader and providing a kind of overview of Spinoza's system. The main body of this *Guide* (Chapter 3) proceeds step-by-step through the *Ethics* – clarifying the terminology, explaining the argument, reflecting on the author's motives and trying to resolve the seeming contradictions. Where Spinoza's text is opaque, I hope that this one will be at least somewhat translucent. Where the going in the *Ethics* is a bit rough, I hope that this *Guide* will be smooth sailing. In Chapter 4 we will trace some of the lines of historical influence reaching from the time of the *Ethics*' publication (in 1678) until today.

The reader's task is challenging, but my hope is that the effort will be rewarded by a greater understanding of an influential philosopher and an important book. The *Ethics* is not an easy work, but as Spinoza famously says – in the very last words of the text – 'all things excellent are as difficult as they are rare'.

The quotations from the *Ethics* have been taken mostly from E. M. Curley's translation, though occasionally from that of Samuel Shirley (see bibliographical details on p. 163 below). I have adopted the now standard shorthand way of referring to passages in the *Ethics*, as indicated by the following examples:

3p17dem refers to the demonstration of proposition 17 of part 3 of the *Ethics*;

2p11c refers to the corollary to proposition 11 of part 2;

1p15s refers to the scholium to proposition 15 of part 1;

2a1 refers to axiom 1 in part 2;

4d1 refers to the first definition of part 4;

L7dem refers to the demonstration of Lemma 7 in the lemmas (all of which are after proposition 13 of Part 2);

Post. 3 refers to third of the Postulates (all of which are after proposition 13 of Part 2);

etc.

CHAPTER 1

SPINOZA AND THE *ETHICS*: BACKGROUND AND CONTEXT

During his lifetime Spinoza was best known for his radical ideas about religion and politics. As a young man of twenty-four he was formally cursed and excommunicated by the Jewish community of Amsterdam because the elders of the synagogue found his views too unorthodox to be tolerated. Fourteen years later, in 1670, he tried to influence the course of events in Dutch politics by publishing a book supporting freedom of thought and freedom of the press. In defending his position he provided an analysis that called into question traditional views of the Bible, institutional religion and the basis of political authority. Even in liberal Holland, such a work could not be published openly, so it appeared anonymously with a title page that falsely claimed that it was printed in Hamburg, Germany. This work, with the imposing title *Theological-Political Treatise*, failed to influence favourably the politics of the day, and was soon widely banned by the authorities. But in spite of the prohibition it was read by intellectuals all over Europe and, when he was eventually identified as the author, Spinoza earned respect as a learned scholar of Biblical texts. Unfortunately he also gained a reputation as a dangerous freethinker and even an atheist.

It was in this atmosphere of notoriety and suspicion that Spinoza finished writing his most important work, the *Ethics*. He had been developing the ideas for this book for many years and had spent the better part of a decade putting the ideas into the clearest and most compelling form he could. He was eager to share his findings and in 1675 actually began negotiations with the publisher. But it became increasingly clear that it would be dangerous for publication to proceed, even anonymously, so he stopped the process and decided to wait for a more auspicious time. He did not live to see that time, though, for within two years Spinoza died at the age of forty-four. The manuscript of the *Ethics* was left in the drawer of his bedside table at his death. It appeared in print the following year in the 'Posthumous Works of B.D.S.', secretly edited and published by his friends. It too was widely banned by the authorities. But it was also widely read.

His earlier work had focused chiefly on religion and political theory, but in the *Ethics* Spinoza broadens the scope of his investigations to address virtually all of the most fundamental issues in philosophy. In one volume he tackles central questions of metaphysics, epistemology, physics, philosophy of mind, psychology and ethics. These questions are not just addressed one after the other, each an isolated puzzle. On the contrary, Spinoza provides a systematic account in which each field of inquiry has its proper place, and each is related to the other fields in a remarkably integrated way.

Though it was suppressed and maligned when it first appeared, Spinoza's *Ethics* is now universally recognized as one of the undisputed masterworks of early modern philosophy. But like many great works, the *Ethics* is not easily accessible for the first-time reader. Spinoza chose to cast his philosophy into geometrical form, beginning with definitions, axioms, propositions and demonstrations. There are good reasons for his choice of this manner of writing (reasons which will be considered in Chapter 3), but the geometrical form does not engage the reader personally in the way that a more conversational or a more narrative style of writing might. The geometrical structure spotlights the philosophical ideas and their logical connections while keeping the author out of sight. The geometrical order of exposition does not give the author a chance to introduce himself or to explain why he is engaged in this philosophical project.

Spinoza preferred to maintain his anonymity, but it is helpful for the modern reader to know something of the author's life and of the circumstances in which he wrote. For one thing, Spinoza's life tells us where his philosophical views lead when put into practice – for he lived his life very much in accordance with the philosophical and moral principles that are found in the *Ethics*. One of the things that most fascinated and puzzled many of his contemporaries was that a man who espoused ideas that seemed so sacrilegious could have lived such a morally exemplary life. Even today the simplicity and calm of his life speak to many of his admirers as eloquently as do his written works. This calm is all the more noteworthy when we recall that he was the target of rejection, hostility and calumny during his life.

SPINOZA'S LIFE

Spinoza was born in 1632 in the bustling port city of Amsterdam, in the Netherlands. The city was at the peak of its power and prosperity at the time, in the midst of what is now referred to as its 'Golden Age'. Commerce was king, and ships arrived every day from all over the world, bringing exotic wares and great wealth to the city. As merchants made their fortunes they built the beautiful patrician houses that still grace the canals of the old city. Amsterdam was home to artists such as Rembrandt (a neighbour of Spinoza's) as well as important scientists such as Anton van Leeuwenhoek, inventor of the microscope.

Perhaps in part because of its role as a centre of international trade, Amsterdam was a progressive and tolerant city – at least by the standards of the time. The city's tolerance of religious diversity is what led Spinoza's forebears to settle there when they were forced to leave their native Portugal. The Spinozas were Jewish, and the Catholic Inquisition offered the Jews in Spain and Portugal only three choices – conversion to Christianity, death or exile. Spinoza's forebears chose exile, sailed to Amsterdam and settled in the city's sizable Jewish Quarter.

Michael and Hana Deborah deSpinoza chose the name 'Baruch' for their eldest son – a Hebrew name meaning 'blessed'. He was educated in the Talmud Torah School, and he might have thought about becoming a rabbi. But as he deepened his study of the Hebrew scriptures and commentaries he found that he agreed less and less with his teachers' orthodox interpretation. He learned about textual interpretation and logic from his study of these works, but ultimately they did not satisfy him.

In his later teenage years (or perhaps his early twenties) his intellectual horizons broadened and he developed a curiosity about the writings of Christian and secular thinkers. In order to read these, though, he had to learn Latin, for almost all such works were written in that language at the time. He found excellent Latin training in the home-school of a physician named Francis van den Enden, and along with the language he began to learn of the larger world of philosophical and scientific ideas.

When Spinoza was twenty years old, his father died. For a while he and his brother Gabriel ran a fruit and vegetable business, but it seems that Spinoza's interests were focused more on his studies than on business. The more he learned, the more his theological and religious views diverged from those of the rabbis and elders. In thought as well as in action Spinoza drifted away from the community, becoming less orthodox in his thinking and less religiously observant in his daily life.

We do not know exactly what led to the final break in 1656. At some point the views that he espoused and the increasingly secular life that he led were judged intolerably unorthodox by the elders. He was offered the opportunity to change his ways and recant his heresies, but he refused to compromise. So, as his ancestors had been driven into exile for religious reasons, Spinoza was exiled from the Jewish community because he refused to conform to the expectations of the orthodox. The ban with which he was formally excommunicated reads (in part) as follows:

> By decree of the angels and by the command of the holy men, we excommunicate, expel, curse and damn Baruch de Espinoza ... Cursed be he by day and cursed be he by night; cursed be he when he lies down and cursed be he when he rises up. Cursed be he when he goes out and cursed be he when he comes in. The Lord will not spare him, but then the anger of the Lord and his jealousy shall smoke against this man, and all the curses that are written in this book shall lie upon him ... [N]o one should communicate with him, neither in writing, nor accord him any favor, nor stay with him under the same roof, nor come within four cubits of him, nor shall he read any treatise composed or written by him.[1]

With these frightful words Spinoza was irrevocably cut off from the community where he had grown up, studied, worked and worshipped.

After his excommunication at the age of twenty-four Spinoza changed his first name, Baruch, to its Latin equivalent, Benedictus. He lived a quiet life, talking sometimes with a group of Protestant

Christians, unorthodox like himself. He exchanged letters with various important businessmen, philosophers and scientists who expressed an interest in his ideas. In the twenty years between his excommunication and his death he moved five times to various cities in the Netherlands, always renting a room in the house of a local citizen. He lived very frugally, supporting himself in modest fashion by grinding lenses. A friend, Simon de Vries, offered to give him two thousand florins (about five hundred pounds Sterling) to make his life easier. But Spinoza asked him to make the gift smaller, explaining that such a large sum would surely distract him from his work and his studies. Rather surprisingly, he was even offered a prestigious and well-paid professorship at the University of Heidelberg in Germany. He politely declined the post, expressing concern about the distractions and political pressures that might accompany such a position.

Spinoza worked away at his lenses and his philosophy in the cramped quarters that were his home. From 1665 to 1670 he set aside the *Ethics* to focus on the *Theological-Political Treatise*. When this was published (as we saw, anonymously and with great controversy) he returned to the main task at hand and worked on the *Ethics* until the end. He was not a recluse in his last years, for a number of learned people valued his insights and came to spend an afternoon in conversation. But he spent most of his time in one room, and the glass dust, that he must have breathed constantly, weakened his lungs. He died quietly of tuberculosis one Sunday afternoon in 1677 in his last home city, The Hague.

THE *ETHICS* AND THE CONTROVERSY

Spinoza had shared some of the content of his *Ethics* with a number of trusted friends over the years. In this way the authorities had come to hear of the fact that that 'renegade Jew' who wrote the pernicious *Treatise* had composed a book in which he intended to present his philosophy in a more comprehensive and systematic way. Upon Spinoza's death, efforts were made to locate the manuscript in order to destroy it or at least to prevent its publication. From as far away as Rome came expressions of concern about the dangerous consequences of allowing the book to see the light of day.[2]

Fortunately Spinoza's friends were able to elude the authorities while they prepared for the printing. The book appeared in January of 1678, and the judgement of the churches and the government was swift and harsh. On the 4 February, within weeks of the first copies appearing, the Reformed Consistory of Leiden pronounced it, 'A book which, perhaps since the beginning of the world until the present day ... surpasses all others in godlessness and endeavours to do away with all religion and set impiety on the throne'. By June the work was officially banned in all of Holland and in most of the rest of the Netherlands.

In order to understand the establishment's fear and opposition to Spinoza's philosophy, it must be remembered that at the time he was writing a gradual but profound intellectual revolution was under way in Western Europe. The outcome was uncertain and the details were unclear, but the general direction of change was pretty obvious. Let us consider some of the most important factors that were driving that revolution.

1. The Renaissance had reawakened awareness of classical culture with its focus on human society and the natural world. And it was not hard to notice that the great authors of the classical age had written brilliantly and insightfully about human life and about the cosmos without benefit of Biblical wisdom or Christian theology.
2. The Reformation had undermined the unity of western Christianity and the unanimity of believers regarding sacraments, salvation and scriptural interpretation. Endless doctrinal controversies and bloody religious wars made it more difficult for thinking people to be quite as confident of the unquestionable truth and rightness of their own beliefs and allegiances.
3. The 'new sciences' of astronomy, optics, and mechanics were questioning the theoretical underpinnings of the Aristotelian–Christian synthesis that had held sway for centuries. As the evidence mounted in favour of Copernicus's view that we are not literally at the centre of the universe, people were led to rethink mankind's 'place' in a more figurative sense. Led by thinkers such as Galileo and Descartes, the new 'natural philosophy' suggested that events in nature occur in accordance with mechanical laws that can be formulated in mathematical terms. As this view gained ground it inevitably raised difficult

questions – about human free will, about the possibility of miracles, and about the role (if any) of purpose – divine purpose – in explaining things. And it was not long before people began to ask whether the sort of mechanical explanations that the new sciences offered could be applied to human beings and to human society as well.

A process of change was under way that would lead ultimately to the Enlightenment and to the worldview that we associate with modernity. A secular outlook based on reason and science would increasingly challenge traditional religious perspectives in debates about human welfare, ethics and politics. Philosophy would become less and less the 'handmaiden of theology' and would instead play an active part in the emergence of the scientific worldview – a worldview that would often be at odds with revealed religion.

In the 1670s this intellectual revolution was still in its earlier stages. Looking back historically though, we can see that the clerics and magistrates were quite right in thinking that Spinoza's works were dangerous. No other work of the time presents such a systematic and coherent vision of how the world might look to someone who is willing to suspend belief in revealed religion and take very seriously the claims of the newly emerging natural science. In Spinoza's works we see the most important characteristics of the Enlightenment and of modernity itself in clear relief. The powers that be were not wrong in thinking that these writings represented a threat to them, for in many ways Spinoza represented the future, and the future was not friendly to their conservative interests.

As we examine the main themes of Spinoza's *Ethics* in the next chapter it will be clear just how radically his views diverged from the mainstream of his day. As we then go through the text itself in more detail we will see how these views fit together in a remarkably integrated system. Though written more than three centuries ago these ideas still have the power to challenge and engage us today.

NOTES

1. A more complete text can be found in Steven Nadler, *Spinoza: A Life*. Cambridge: Cambridge University Press, 1999, p. 120.
2. For an excellent discussion of the controversy surrounding the publication of the *Ethics*, see Jonathan Israel's, *Radical Enlightenment*. Oxford: Oxford University Press, 2001. The quoted passage from the Leiden Consistory is found in Israel's work (p. 291).

CHAPTER 2

MAIN THEMES AND INFLUENCES

In the *Ethics* Spinoza provides an account of reality as a whole and an explanation of how human beings fit into that larger reality. The details of his argument, presented in geometrical form and couched in metaphysical language, can be difficult to follow. (We will try in Chapter 3 to clear a path through that thicket.) But the main ideas that constitute the broad contours of his philosophy are not really difficult at all. On the contrary, these ideas are clear, and they fit together to form a consistent and (in many ways) appealing worldview. If we can get clear on the big picture, the details will be much more accessible.

It is at the level of the big ideas, too, that we can most easily note the influence of earlier thinkers on Spinoza. The geometrical form of writing obscures the extent to which Spinoza is addressing issues that had been raised by previous philosophers and were topics of active controversy in his day. Spinoza almost never mentions other philosophers in the *Ethics*, but the knowledgeable reader can see signs of the ancient Stoics in Spinoza's ethical doctrines and traces of Hobbes in his political theory. The biblical critique in the *Theological-Political Treatise* owes much to Maimonides and other Jewish scholars. In his letters Spinoza readily grants the influence that the ancient atomists (Democritus and Lucretius) had on his thinking. Like all other philosophers, Spinoza was implicitly in conversation with the tradition – he was inspired and provoked by the questions and claims of a number of earlier writers.

The single thinker whose ideas most directly influenced Spinoza was the French philosopher René Descartes. A creative mathematician and a founder of modern philosophy, Descartes developed a system that he hoped would provide a grounding for the new

MAIN THEMES AND INFLUENCES

mathematically based physical sciences while reconciling those new sciences with the most important tenets of Christianity. His philosophy offered an alternative to the Aristotelian/Scholastic system that had dominated Western thought for centuries. He presented his new ideas in a series of writings in the 1630s and 1640s, and though he died in 1650 his ideas grew steadily more influential in the following decades.

It was the 1650s when Spinoza, as a young adult, learned Latin in the school of Francis van den Enden and began to read the works of Christian and secular philosophers. Descartes' works, which were setting the intellectual agenda for progressive thinkers all over Europe, influenced the educational agenda for the young Spinoza as well. Along with Latin, Spinoza learned the basics of Descartes' philosophy. He became such an expert that for a while he had private students of his own who came to him specifically to study the philosophy of Descartes. In fact, Spinoza recast one of Descartes' works (*The Principles of Philosophy*) into geometrical form in order to aid one of his students in learning the ideas. Some friends later persuaded Spinoza to publish this teaching-aid – it was the only work that Spinoza was able to publish openly during his lifetime.

Descartes' ideas influenced Spinoza's *Ethics* profoundly, but this influence does not show up as widespread agreement on basic doctrines. On the contrary, Spinoza disagrees with Descartes on some of the most central issues in philosophy. As we consider the main themes of the *Ethics* we can often see them as responses to and correctives for what Spinoza took to be fundamental errors in the new Cartesian philosophy. We will look at four of the central and most original ideas that made the *Ethics* such a groundbreaking and controversial work. In doing so, we will set up the context for understanding the fine-structure of the text (in Chapter 3) and will also note, in passing, the extent of Spinoza's disagreement with the most influential philosopher of his day.

1. GOD

God plays an absolutely central role in Spinoza's philosophical system. This is not in itself unusual, of course. It was true of medieval philosophy and of Descartes' new system as well. What *is* unusual is that Spinoza develops and defends a wholly novel account of what God is. His God is not the heavenly Father of the Judaeo-Christian tradition. On the contrary, Spinoza argues that God must encompass everything that exists. God is the cause of all things, but not in the sense that he created things separate from himself. Rather, God is in all things and all things are in God. In fact, according to Spinoza, every single thing in the world is a part of God – a manifestation of the active presence of God in and as that thing. Because God includes everything that exists, Spinoza sometimes directly equates God with nature, suggesting that these are just two words that refer to the same reality.

The *Ethics* is divided into five parts. The first of these (entitled 'De Deo' – 'On God') is devoted entirely to deducing, explaining and defending this unusual conception of God. The first section (Propositions 1–15) uses abstract metaphysical terms widely employed by philosophers in the seventeenth century (e.g. 'substance,' 'attribute,' 'mode') to present a rational argument that this God must exist and that only this God can possibly exist. The central propositions of this part of the work clarify how all things follow from God and explain the causal process by which things come into being. The Appendix to this part – one of the best-known sections of the *Ethics* – explains, in a non-technical way, why the true nature of God has been so widely misunderstood through the ages.

In offering this very different account of God Spinoza is of course implicitly criticizing traditional theology and the scriptural sources on which the traditional conception is largely based. If God is identical with all of nature, then God clearly does not have any of the personal, human-like characteristics attributed to God in the Judaeo-Christian tradition. For example, God has no face or voice – no emotions, desires, purposes or will (as we normally understand these terms). In the *Theological-Political Treatise* Spinoza provides a careful and lengthy analysis and critique of the Bible and of the way in which religious believers have been misled in their understanding of the nature of God. In the *Ethics* he does not linger over these questions, but he makes it clear that in order to gain an adequate understanding of God and of human beings' place in the world the reader will have to recognize that the traditional anthropomorphic 'personal' conception of God is false.

Spinoza's novel conception of God is, as mentioned, central for his entire philosophy. Indeed, this conception is so ubiquitous in Spinoza's thinking that a poet of a later century referred to him as a

'God-intoxicated man'. But in the opinion of the clerics and magistrates of his own day, Spinoza's God was no God at all, and they did not hesitate to accuse him of atheism, pure and simple. In fact, for decades after his death, to charge someone with 'Spinozism' was just another way of calling that person an atheist. The reader will have to decide whether Spinoza's God deserves the name. But we will be in a better position to make that judgement after a more detailed study of Part 1 of the *Ethics* (in Chapter 3 of this *Reader's Guide*).

2. UNIVERSAL CAUSAL DETERMINISM

A kind of corollary to the view that all things are parts of God is the idea that all things in nature fit together in an orderly and structured whole. According to Spinoza, this is a causal order – things and events are caused by other things and events in accordance with the laws of nature (which might also be called the structuring principles of the divine Being). Every event in nature is caused by prior events and conditions, and every event has consequences (effects) of its own. There is a kind of ineluctable necessity built into this notion, for without the causes the effect cannot exist, and if the causes are present, the effect must necessarily follow. This view is often referred to as 'causal determinism'. Spinoza was as resolute a causal determinist as any philosopher has ever been.

It is easy to see how universal causal determinism would appeal to a philosopher interested in supporting the new natural science that was being developed by Galileo, Descartes and others in the seventeenth century. But there were many thinkers who found the doctrine unacceptable because it seemed to pose a threat to certain religious and moral doctrines. If every event in nature is caused by a prior event, in accordance with the laws of nature, there seems to be no place for the miracles attested to in the Bible. Miracles were taken to represent momentary incursions of the supernatural into the course of natural events – bringing about results that would not normally follow in the natural order. It seemed difficult to reconcile such miracles with universal causal determinism. Many religious thinkers thus rejected determinism. But Spinoza, who after all denied that there is anything outside nature, embraced determinism and rejected miracles of the supernatural kind.

A different kind of objection to determinism came from those concerned about its ethical implications. If every thing and every occurrence in nature is the necessary result of prior causes, then human actions must also be causally determined like every other event. But if that is the case, then our choices and our decisions are the ineluctable effects of prior causal factors, and given those causes our choices could not have been different from what they were. This seems to rule out human free will, and that would seem to undermine our notions of moral responsibility. If my sinful or criminal act was the necessary result of prior causes, how can I justly be held responsible for it?

Descartes had found this implication so troubling that he ultimately rejected determinism. Though he favoured the view that the entire physical world acts in accordance with the causal laws of nature, he made an exception for the human mind. According to Descartes human beings possess a free will that is not subject to the laws of nature. This will is such that its decisions and actions are not determined by prior causes, but are the product of completely free and unconditioned choice. Since the decisions of this free will do not have causes, as do all other events in nature, they are not part of a single universal deterministic causal system that can ultimately be understood in terms of the new science of nature. Despite his commitment to this new science, Descartes was willing to draw a line and to exclude the human mind from its purview. To ensure that we have free will Descartes made the human mind an exception to the (otherwise universal) laws of nature.

Spinoza would have none of this. According to him, human beings and their actions, are, one and all, part of nature and are subject to the same causal laws that govern all natural events. He even explicitly ridicules the Cartesian view, saying that it makes every human being a 'kingdom within a kingdom'. According to Spinoza there is only one 'kingdom' (nature) and every event in that kingdom happens in accordance with the laws of nature. He develops this view in the central sections of Part 1 of the *Ethics*, and late in Part 2 (Propositions 48 & 49) he explicitly argues that human beings do not constitute an exception to the universal causal determinism. Spinoza accepts, as an implication of his view, that there is no free will. But he argues in the latter parts of the *Ethics* that there is a more important and more valuable kind of freedom that can be achieved by human beings by means of understanding ourselves as parts of nature.

MAIN THEMES AND INFLUENCES

3. THE MIND AND BODY

Concerned, in part, to ensure a place for free will, Descartes declared that the human mind is not part of the causal order. But he was quite interested in and supportive of the new natural sciences of mechanics, optics and astronomy, so he wanted to grant that there is universal causation in the world at large. How to uphold universal causation in the world studied by the sciences while denying that the mind can be understood in causal terms? Descartes solved (or avoided) this problem by maintaining that the mind is an entirely different kind of thing from the material world. On this view, the material universe consists of one physical substance, characterized by infinite extension in space. In addition to this physical substance there exist minds – mental substances characterized by conscious thinking and possessing the power of making choices and willing. A human being, in Descartes' theory, consists of (1) a body that is a part of the extended substance and (2) a mind that thinks and wills.

This is Descartes' famous 'dualism' – the view that human beings consist of a mind and a body, and that the mind and body are fundamentally different kinds of things. This is in many ways a common-sensical view, presupposed in our everyday ways of talking as well as in the theories of many earlier philosophers. But in one of his most radical departures from tradition, Spinoza explicitly denies this dualistic view. According to Spinoza, the mental and the physical – the mind and the body – are not two different kinds of things, but rather two different ways of understanding and describing one single thing. This view is explained and defended in the early sections of Part 2 of the *Ethics*. We will discuss it in more detail below. In the remainder of Part 2 Spinoza makes use of his theory of the identity of mind and body in explaining how we can acquire knowledge of ourselves and the world – and why we so often fall into error. This view of the mind and the body also provides the conceptual underpinnings for the investigation of the emotions.

4. A LIBERATING SCIENCE OF HUMAN EMOTIONS

Thinkers who are interested in ethics and in moral psychology – from the ancients to the most contemporary theorists – must necessarily consider the role of the emotions in human experience and conduct. The emotions (especially those that are traditionally classified as 'passions') are usually viewed as non-rational and very often as excessive and destructive. The ethical task is then to 'tame' these passions by bringing them under the control of 'right reason'. Spinoza, too, is interested in the relation between reason and the passions, but his approach focuses not on taming these wayward emotions, but on liberating ourselves from their destructive power by gaining an understanding of them. To this end, he develops a systematic science of the emotions (in Part 3 of the *Ethics*). Then, in the final sections of the work (Parts 4 and 5) Spinoza employs this science of the emotions to explain what a strong and joyful human life would be, and to outline a therapeutic programme that leads (as he says) from bondage to liberation. By coming to understand ourselves and our emotions as parts of nature, we can achieve a kind of joy and freedom that Spinoza calls 'blessedness'.

Having begun with a radically unorthodox conception of God, Spinoza leads the reader to a kind of secular salvation through rational self-understanding. Key to this programme for liberation is the fact that we human beings are parts of God, i.e. parts of the natural order that, like all other things and events in nature, can be understood in terms of causes and effects. According to Spinoza, to know ourselves in this way brings a cessation of emotional upheaval, a clarity of perspective and a calm satisfaction of mind. It fosters a reverence for nature and a joyful appreciation of nature's power, order and diversity. In the closing pages of the *Ethics* Spinoza does not hesitate to identify this reverence and this joy as a kind of beatitude – a profound and timeless experience of the love of God.

These are the main themes of the *Ethics*. They are not really difficult to comprehend, but to follow the development of these themes in a detailed and systematic way, presented as they are in geometrical form, can be a challenge for the modern reader. In the next chapter we will reflect briefly on this geometrical method of exposition, and then move step-by-step through this masterwork, providing the background information and textual analysis to make it clear and accessible for us today.

CHAPTER 3

READING THE TEXT

As its title suggests, Spinoza's most important work is a treatise on ethics. But the subject matter is 'ethics' in the sense in which the ancients used the term. When Aristotle, the Stoics or the Epicureans investigated the subject of ethics they were seeking to discover what is the best kind of life for a human being, and how we can live that kind of life.

Spinoza explains, in an unfinished work entitled *Treatise on the Emendation of the Intellect*, that as a young man he had come to the realization that the kinds of things that people pursue in the hope of achieving happiness (wealth, physical pleasures, fame) are often vain and empty. At best they are temporarily satisfying; at worst they are obsessive and destructive. Spinoza wanted something more deeply and permanently satisfying than a life spent in the pursuit of these problematic pleasures. So he undertook to discover if there was a better way to live – 'if there was something which, once found and acquired, would continuously give [him] the greatest joy, to eternity'. He implies that he found what he was looking for, and in the process identified the best way for a human being to live. The *Ethics* tells us what he discovered.

As might be expected from a philosopher, Spinoza emphasizes the importance of knowledge – and more specifically self-knowledge – for achieving the good life. But we human beings are a part and product of nature, and hence in order to understand ourselves we must understand the basic principles of nature. This too is very much in the tradition of the ancient ethicists. But Spinoza's account departs from ancient precedent as he develops in detail his conception of nature and of mankind as a part of nature.

The *Ethics* is divided into five parts. The first of these deals with

God or nature and how the world of finite things follows from the infinite and eternal God. Part 2 introduces the human mind, explaining how we come to know what we know, and how we so often go astray in our thinking. In Part 3 Spinoza develops a detailed theory of the emotions, while Part 4 explains what kind of emotional life is conducive to a life of strength and happiness. Finally, in the fifth part we learn how reason and understanding can help to overcome destructive passions, and even provide a kind of blessedness and (as Spinoza calls it) 'salvation'. This is the culmination of the ethical doctrine.

Spinoza's views on God and on blessedness are closely related. He holds that we must overcome the prejudices and illusions of traditional theology if we are to gain the insight that makes blessedness possible. So the order of ideas themselves dictates the order in which they must be considered – first God, then human beings and their blessedness.

PART 1 – ON GOD

The first part of the *Ethics* lays out Spinoza's unusual conception of God and provides an explanation of the way in which the world is 'in' God, is caused by God and follows from God. The early pages are among the densest and most difficult to understand in all of Western philosophy. The general outline is pretty clear, but the detailed step-by-step arguments can be nearly impenetrable. In what follows we will provide a somewhat simplified version of the argument contained in the first fourteen propositions of this part. The simplification will not distort Spinoza's intentions, but it will make the argument more accessible for the first-time reader. For the rest of Part 1 we will remain quite close to the text, focusing on specific propositions and trying to follow Spinoza's reasoning in a little more detail.

We will begin to work our way into the arguments of the opening sections by taking a look first at the odd manner in which Spinoza chose to write.

The geometrical method of demonstration

A great part of the difficulty in understanding Spinoza's greatest work results from the way he wrote it – the actual structure of the exposition. Upon opening the *Ethics* the reader first notices not the controversial ideas but the unusual way Spinoza writes. First come definitions, then axioms, then a number of propositions, each one followed by a proof. The model for this kind of writing is Euclid's classical text from the third century BCE, entitled *The Elements of Geometry*. Spinoza presents his philosophical views as if he were writing a treatise on mathematics. He calls this form of writing the 'geometrical method of demonstration', and its concise formality has intimidated many a first-time reader.[1]

The geometrical method of demonstration does not smooth the path for easy reading, but there are good reasons why Spinoza chose this unusual way of writing – reasons rooted in his philosophy and in the age in which he wrote. It will help to ease our transition into the text itself if we focus for a moment on the reasons for Spinoza's choice of this unconventional way of presenting his ideas.

The Renaissance had brought a renewal of interest in the ancient mathematicians, and the importance of geometry for artists of that period is obvious. (Think of the converging lines of Raphael's *School of Athens* or of Leonardo's Vitruvian Man, with the human figure inscribed in both a circle and a square.) But the seventeenth century – during which Spinoza lived and died – was imbued with an even more profound respect for mathematics. In the early part of the century Galileo applied mathematics to the study of nature with spectacular results. In fact, in a famous passage Galileo declared that mathematics is the very language of nature itself:

> Philosophy is written in this grand book – the universe – which stands continuously open to our gaze. But the book cannot be understood unless one first learns to comprehend the language and read the letters in which it is composed. It is written in the language of mathematics, and its characters are triangles, circles and other geometric figures, without which it is humanly impossible to understand a single word of it; without these one wanders about in a dark labyrinth.[2]

Galileo had shown that mathematics (especially geometry) can very successfully describe and explain natural phenomena. In the seventeenth century mathematics itself seemed to be the perfect example of real knowledge – of clear and indubitable knowledge. In Euclidean geometry, for example, everything follows with complete deductive certainty from the initial premises: if we once grasp and accept the definitions, axioms and postulates, the truth of the propositions derived from them is beyond doubt. Spinoza believed that any well-ordered system of real knowledge could be put into this sort of geometrical order with self-evident axioms and definitions, and deductively certain theorems derived from them.

In Chapter 2 we noted that Spinoza actually put the principles of Descartes' philosophy into geometrical order in order to make it easier for his students to understand. At the encouragement of several friends, he agreed to have the work published. The Preface to that volume, written by Spinoza's friend Lodewijk Meyer, offers the following explanation of the importance of the geometrical method:

> It is the unanimous opinion of all who seek wisdom beyond the common lot that the best and surest way to discover and to teach truth is the method used by mathematicians in their study and exposition of the sciences, namely that whereby conclusions are demonstrated from definitions, postulates and axioms. And indeed rightly so. Because all sure and sound knowledge of what is unknown can be elicited and derived only from what is already known with certainty, this latter must first be built up from the ground as a solid foundation on which thereafter to construct the entire edifice of human knowledge, if that is not to collapse of its own accord or give way at the slightest blow.[3]

Spinoza wants his philosophy to have the kind of clarity and solidity that comes from mathematical demonstration. And so he presents his entire systematic account of reality and of our place in reality in geometrical form. The result is a challenging and difficult work, but Spinoza is confident that the reader's pains will be rewarded by the pleasures of clear insight and sure understanding.

There is also a further reason why Spinoza chooses to present his philosophy in the geometrical manner. When historians of philosophy place thinkers into categories, Spinoza is usually classified as a 'rationalist'. Generally speaking, rationalists believe that if we start with really clear, simple and certainly true ideas, and if we then proceed carefully in a deductive manner, drawing out the consequences of these ideas, we can arrive at a whole series of truths which accurately reflect reality itself. This is just what Euclid did –

he began with clear and simple definitions and self-evident axioms, and then deduced from these a whole systematic series of geometrical truths. If the reader has any doubts about a later proposition in Euclid's system, it is always possible to trace the proposition back to its grounding in the initial premises. These premises – the definitions, axioms and postulates – were thought to be so obvious and indubitable that they required no further justification. They were self-justifying.

Spinoza wants his philosophy to have this kind of solid grounding, complete intelligibility and thorough rational justification at all levels. He thinks that if he presents his system in geometrical form, the solidity of the foundation will be manifest and the logical relations by which the rest of the system follows from that initial foundation will be clear. To organize an entire philosophical system into geometrical order is an incredibly ambitious undertaking, and Spinoza spent years of his life working out the details. The result is a very carefully constructed edifice of ideas that strikes most readers as impressive – but somewhat fearsome. We can ask later whether Spinoza achieved the clarity and compelling persuasiveness that he sought. Let us first try to follow his reasoning at the outset of the *Ethics*. Let us take a look at how he begins.

The concept of substance

The *Ethics* is divided into five parts. The first of these is entitled simply *De Deo* ('Of God'). The reader might expect that the focus of attention, from the beginning, would be upon God. But in fact that is not the case at all. One of the eight definitions at the beginning of Part 1 offers us a version of the meaning of the term 'God', but after that we hear not a word about God until nearly a third of the way into Part 1 (i.e. until the eleventh proposition out of a total of 36 propositions in this part). Instead, the focus in the first ten propositions is on the notion of 'substance'. Spinoza establishes a number of claims about substance and then, in Proposition 11, brings God back in by claiming that God is identical to the 'substance' that he has been discussing in the first ten propositions. Why does he proceed in this way?

This question can best be answered by looking again at geometry as a model of clear and rational understanding. We saw that in Euclid's *Elements* each theorem rests on prior theorems, and that ultimately the whole series of truths rests on the definitions and axioms of the system – which are taken to be self-evident and hence not in need of further explanation or justification. Thus every claim at every level is fully justified – either by previously proven propositions or (in the case of each of the initial premises) by its own self-evidence. As we noted before, Spinoza wants his entire philosophy to have this kind of rationally structured intelligibility.

According to Spinoza, the reader of Euclid does not really understand a proposition until she understands how that proposition was derived from the earlier propositions (and ultimately from the definitions and axioms at the basis of the system). On this view, if Proposition B is entailed and justified by Proposition A, then I do not really understand B unless I understand A and understand how B follows logically from A. In geometry the relation between an earlier proposition and a later one is a logical relation. Among things and events in the world, the relations are causal relations. Spinoza thinks of causal relations in a way that is very similar to logical relations. For example, he thinks that we do not really understand something unless and until we understand its cause. He states, as an axiom, 'The knowledge of an effect depends on, and involves, the knowledge of its cause' (Axiom 4). We noted in the last chapter that Spinoza believes that every thing and every event has a cause – that all things follow in a causal order in accordance with the laws of nature. A version of this causal principle is also stated as an axiom (Axiom 3) – i.e. as something so obvious that it requires no argument or justification: 'From a given determinate cause the effect follows necessarily; and conversely, if there is no determinate cause, it is impossible for an effect to follow.'

Spinoza conceives of a world in which effects follow from their causes in orderly ways and in which an effect can be understood by understanding its cause. That cause, in turn, can be understood by understanding its cause – and so on. We can trace the causes of something by going back through the series of prior causes just as, in reading Euclid, we can trace the justification for a given theorem back through the series of prior propositions. In the case of geometry, however, we eventually arrive at the ultimate starting points from which all else follows – the definitions and axioms that require no further justification and can serve to ground the entire system. If Spinoza's philosophical account of reality is to have the same kind of fully rational intelligibility as geometry, there must be a starting point for the system – something that requires no further cause in order to exist and requires no further explanation in order to be understood. This is the starting point that Spinoza's philosophy requires. To put it more strongly (and Spinoza would want to put it more strongly) this is the starting point that is required if reality is to be rationally intelligible. There must be something that can exist without a prior cause – an explanatory principle that requires no further explanation. The term Spinoza uses to refer to this starting point is 'substance'.

'Substance' is a term that has long been at the heart of that branch of philosophy known as metaphysics. It is an age-old concept whose meaning has changed in various ways through the ages. The sense in which Spinoza employs the term is similar to the way Descartes uses it. Descartes defines the term 'substance' this way: 'A substance is a thing that so exists that it needs no other thing in order to exist.' This is the starting point that Spinoza needs. By definition substance requires no prior cause in order to exist. And since it has no prior cause, we can know and understand it without having to understand its cause.

Spinoza's own definition of 'substance' will require some more clarification, but the basic idea is the same. The third definition of Part 1 of the *Ethics* reads, 'By substance I understand what is in itself and is conceived through itself, that is, that whose concept does not require the concept of another thing, from which it must be formed.' While the idea is pretty clear here, the terminology demands some explanation.

Spinoza's definition includes two kinds of claims – an ontological claim and a conceptual claim. When he says that substance is 'in itself' he is making an ontological claim. For Spinoza, to say that one thing (B) is 'in' another (A) is to say (among other things) that B is ontologically dependent on A. Ontological dependence is an abstract metaphysical notion, but it can be clarified by means of an example. Think about the relationship between a face and a smile. A face is ontologically more fundamental than a smile. There can be faces without smiles, but there cannot be smiles without faces (stories of Cheshire cats notwithstanding!). Faces underlie smiles. Smiles are ontologically dependent on faces. In Spinoza's terminology we would say that smiles are 'in' faces.

To pursue this example further, we should note that in order to think of a smile, one must think of a face. Indeed, a smile just is a certain modification of a face – a certain configuration of the features of a face. In order to conceive of a smile one must necessarily also conceive of a face. This kind of relationship can be called a conceptual dependence – smiles are conceptually dependent on faces.

To return to Spinoza's definition of substance – when he says that a substance is 'in itself' he means that it is not ontologically dependent on anything else. When he says that it is 'that whose concept does not require the concept of any other thing, from which it must be formed', he is saying that a substance is not conceptually dependent on anything else. It requires nothing else in order to be, and in order to conceive it we do not have to conceive anything else. A substance is thus ontologically and conceptually ultimate. In this sense, it is like the definitions and axioms of geometry – they do not follow from anything else, but everything else follows from them. That is what Spinoza means by substance – and substance is the starting point of his system.

Study questions

1. What is about geometry that makes it (in the eyes of seventeenth-century philosophers) a paradigm case of full rational understanding?
2. Explain the notions of ontological dependency and conceptual dependency.
3. Is it true that in order for reality to be rationally understandable there must be something that requires no further explanation and is not caused by anything beyond itself?

Substance – necessary, infinite, singular, indivisible, divine (Part 1, Propositions 1–14)

The first few propositions of Part 1 of the *Ethics* are very difficult to follow in detail. The steps of the argument are formulated in terms for which Spinoza has offered formal definitions, but the reader is not yet really in a position to understand these terms. The best way to proceed, when first reading the text, is to focus on the overall structure and the main conclusions of this initial argumentation. When the general outline of Spinoza's thinking is more firmly in place, the reader can return to the specifics of these first propositions with a better chance of following the argument.

READING THE TEXT

Spinoza's strategy is to start with the concept of a substance and show what follows from the fact that it is 'in itself and conceived through itself'. He draws an extensive list of conclusions about substance – conclusions that will have profound implications for the rest of his account of reality. Ultimately, he finds that there can only be one substance – only one thing that is not dependent on anything else. Once he has established that there can be only *one* such thing, he shows that everything else is ultimately caused by and dependent upon that one substance. In fact, all things in the world are manifestations of the one first cause.

Spinoza arrives at this sweeping conclusion by analysing the very idea of substance – by following out the logical implications of the definition. Let us briefly follow the basic outline of his argument. First he shows that no substance could possibly be caused or produced by another. This is because if substance B were caused by substance A, then in order to conceive of B we would have to conceive of its cause A (by Axiom 4 that tells us that knowledge of an effect depends on and involves knowledge of the cause). But if conceiving of B requires conceiving of A, then B is not conceived 'through itself' and is hence not a substance. So no substance can be caused by another. (This is the alternative proof that Spinoza offers for Proposition 6.)

It is axiomatic for Spinoza that whatever cannot be conceived through another must be conceived through itself (Axiom 2). And since being 'conceived through' something is related to being caused by that thing, Spinoza concludes that since a substance cannot be caused by anything else, it must be its own cause (*causa sui*) (1p7d). This is an odd notion, especially for contemporary readers. When we think of causation nowadays, we think of the cause as occurring before the effect. But if the cause temporally precedes the effect, how could something be its own cause? Obviously something cannot temporally precede itself!

This is another point at which it is clear that Spinoza thinks of causation in a way that is different from our contemporary notion. We noted earlier that Spinoza thinks of causal relations in a way that is similar to logical relations. Geometry will again provide the best example of what Spinoza has in mind. The nature of a triangle is such that its angles always add up to 180 degrees. Spinoza would say that the nature of a triangle 'causes' it to be true that the angles equal 180 degrees. But there is no time relationship here. The nature of a triangle does not *temporally* precede the fact that its angles equal 180 degrees. The relationship is one of logical implication – it 'follows from' the nature of a triangle that its angles total 180 degrees, but this 'following from' does not involve time. The relationship is like the relationship which holds between the premises and the conclusion of a valid argument. The conclusion follows from the premises, but there is no time involved.

In a similar way, Spinoza says that the existence of a substance follows from its very nature or essence. Proposition 7 tells us that 'It pertains to the nature of a substance to exist.' This is what is meant by saying that substance is *causa sui*. According to Spinoza a nonexistent substance is inconceivable, in the same way that it is inconceivable that the angles of a Euclidean triangle not total 180 degrees. A substance's existence follows necessarily (and in a way that has no reference to time) from its own nature.

In the very next proposition (1p8) Spinoza deduces that 'Every substance is necessarily infinite.' No formal definition of 'infinite' has been provided, but the straightforward reading of 'infinite' as meaning 'without limit' is all the argument requires. If a substance were limited, it would have to be limited by something else – after all, it could not be limited by nothing. But if it were limited by something else, then that other thing would be (at least in part) the cause of the substance's being what it is. But that is impossible, since no substance can be caused by anything else. Thus, a substance cannot be limited, and hence must be infinite.

Until this point Spinoza has been writing as if there might be a number of substances. Just before Proposition 11, however, he makes it clear that this was just a provisional way of speaking. 'But if someone now asks by what sign we shall be able to distinguish the diversity of substances, let him read the following propositions, which show that in nature there exists only one substance, and that it is absolutely infinite. So that sign would be sought in vain.' An infinite substance can have no boundaries and have no limitations. Nothing can lie outside it, and hence it must be all-inclusive. And if it is indeed *all* inclusive, there can be no other. There is only one substance.

The argument that we have been tracing is a much-simplified version of the argument that Spinoza develops in the first ten propositions of the *Ethics*. A number of technicalities and difficulties have been ignored here, but the general line of argument is intact. In order to advance to the next stage, though, we must introduce a couple of the terms that we have intentionally disregarded until now. The first of these is the term 'attribute'.

Initially Spinoza's official definition does not seem very helpful. 'By attribute I understand what the intellect perceives of a substance, as constituting its essence.' Spinoza uses this notion of an attribute in the complex proof for the uniqueness and infinity of substance here at the beginning of the work, but the reader does not really discover exactly what he has in mind until Part 2 of the *Ethics*, in which the concept of the attributes plays a crucial role. In Part 1 the idea remains quite abstract.

The essence of a thing is its fundamental nature – that which is most characteristic and most fundamentally expressive of what it is. In the case of a substance, if the essence reflects the substance's fundamental nature, the essence must be such that its concept does not require the concept of anything else from which it must be formed. (The definition of substance demands this, and Proposition 10 reiterates the point.) We will learn in Part 2 that spatial extension is one of the ways that we can think of the essence of substance. Spinoza holds that an individual extended thing, such as a tree, must be 'conceived through' extension itself – i.e. we must think of a tree as a certain configuration of extension – as an extended thing. To think of a tree we must 'conceive it through' extension – much as we suggested earlier that in order to think of a smile we must 'conceive it through' a face. But extension is special because, according to Spinoza, we do not have to conceive extension itself through anything further. In this sense, extension is conceptually ultimate. The fact that it does not have to be conceived through anything else tells us that we have reached bedrock – i.e. that we have reached the ultimacy that is definitive of substance – the essence of substance. Since our intellect regards extension as constituting the essence of substance, extension is (by Definition 4) an attribute of substance.

Spinoza holds that just as individual extended things are 'in' and 'conceived through' the attribute of *extension*, so too individual ideas and mental states are 'in' and must be 'conceived through' the general category of *thought*. A specific idea is, so to speak, a certain configuration of thought. Since thought itself does not require any further concept through which it must be conceived, we can recognize it too as conceptually ultimate, and hence as an attribute of substance. These two attributes – extension and thought – are central to Spinoza's overall account of reality, and we will examine them more closely when we come to Part 2 of the *Ethics*. Here in Part 1, however, Spinoza is just concerned to make the point that although there might be more than one category that is conceptually ultimate – i.e. more than one way that we can conceive of the essence of substance – that does not mean that there is more than one substance. Descartes, who argued that there are two distinct kinds of substances (the famous Cartesian dualism) seems to have fallen into this error. But Spinoza avoids dualism, for he has an independent argument (sketched above) for the claim that there can be only one substance. He grants that extension and thought are both conceptually ultimate, but holds that they are nonetheless both attributes of the one single substance.

Having established that there is one infinite, necessarily existent substance, and that that substance is not limited to a single attribute, Spinoza reasons that that boundless substance must have an infinite number of attributes, and that each of these must itself be infinite. In Proposition 11 he brings all of these claims together and introduces, for the first time, the term 'God'. 'God, or a substance consisting of infinite attributes, each of which expresses eternal and infinite essence, necessarily exists.' With this proposition Spinoza establishes, in the abstract, the conceptual basis for his system and the ontological basis for reality. Now he can begin to explain how the world as we know and experience it is related to this metaphysical foundation.

Study question

1. Spinoza starts with the definition of 'substance' as that which is in itself and conceived through itself, and shows that substance must be its own cause, that it must be infinite and that there can be only one substance. Trace the basic outlines of the argument.

Two questions regarding Proposition 11
But before we proceed we should consider two issues raised by Proposition 11. The first of these issues concerns the doctrine of the attributes; the second concerns Spinoza's use of the term 'God'. Let us look at these in turn.

READING THE TEXT

Though we know only two attributes (extension and thought), Spinoza claims that there are infinite attributes, each of which is itself infinite. Even in Spinoza's own day, friends and correspondents with whom he shared his views found this doctrine perplexing. The idea that one reality (substance or God) could have two essences that are as different from each other as extension and thought, seems puzzling. And the notion that it might have an infinite number of such essences – of which we seem for some mysterious reason to know only two – seems even harder to fathom. Some have sought to make sense of this view by focusing on the definition of 'attribute', noting that Spinoza does not say that an attribute is the essence of a substance, but that an attribute is 'what the intellect perceives of a substance, as constituting its essence'. The wording of this definition seems to leave room for a distinction between the real essence and 'what the intellect perceives as constituting' the essence. On this view, the infinity of the attributes might somehow be a function of how the intellect perceives things. Assuming that 'the intellect' in question is the human intellect, there might be something in the way the human intellect perceives that gives rise to the appearance of differentiation where there is really unity – or the appearance of multiplicity where there is really singularity. On this view, sometimes called the 'subjective' interpretation of the attributes, the distinction among the attributes is merely apparent. Other scholars of Spinoza's works have held that the attributes are not merely a subjective result of the way the intellect perceives things, but that the distinction among them must be taken as real.

The infinity of attributes is a complex and obscure doctrine whose difficulties plague any attempt at a consistent interpretation of this aspect of Spinoza's thought. These problems will not be resolved here. Fortunately, this particular doctrine is not centrally important in the further development of the system. When we consider Spinoza's theory of the human mind and its relation to the body (early in Part 2 of the *Ethics*) we will gain greater clarity about the connections between the two known attributes, and this will be important. But the doctrine of the infinity of the attributes will play no further role in the *Ethics* and can be safely left aside.

The second important question raised by Proposition 11 concerns Spinoza's use of the term 'God'. Why – and by what right – does he use this name for the substance whose existence he seeks to demonstrate in the opening propositions of his main philosophical work? More orthodox believers from his time to the present have objected that his *substance* has very little in common with the divine personage of traditional theism and that his appropriation of the term 'God' for that substance is thus misleading. These critics are certainly correct in saying that Spinoza's God differs radically from the deity of the Judaeo-Christian tradition. As we will see, going forward, he highlights especially those characteristics that differentiate his God from that of the Hebrew Bible or the New Testament. Why then did he use the name?

The simplest answer that Spinoza can offer (and the answer that he does offer in the demonstration of Proposition 11) is to point to his definition of God (Definition 5): 'By God I understand a being absolutely infinite – i.e. a substance consisting of an infinity of attributes, of which each one expresses an eternal and infinite essence.' By this definition, the term 'God' is entirely appropriate for the substance whose existence he just finished proving in the first ten propositions of the *Ethics*. But this answer of course begs the question against those who would argue that his definition, with all its metaphysical abstraction, fails to capture the most important characteristics of the deity.

We will be in a better position to judge this issue when we have looked more closely at Spinoza's account of the relation between his God and the ordinary things of the world. But already, in his defense, we could point out that in most mature theological traditions there have been thinkers who have sought to improve our understanding of God by using concepts and ideas from philosophy. Very often they have focused on God's status as ontologically ultimate, noting His infinity, unity, omnipresence, omniscience and timelessness. There is then often a tension between this intellectual and somewhat abstract conception of God and the decidedly more anthropomorphic deity of the *Bible*. Spinoza's God may not have much in common with Jehovah, but he is certainly a recognizable variant of what has been called the 'God of the philosophers'.

Propositions 12 and 13 return to the terminology of 'substance' to argue that the infinite substance whose existence he has proven is indivisible. The proof is in the form of a dilemma: if substance were divided, then the parts into which it is divided would have to be either substances or not substances. If they were substances, then

READING THE TEXT

there would be more than one substance (which he has shown to be impossible). If the parts into which the substance is divided were not themselves substances, then the initial substance would have ceased to be (which Spinoza has shown to be impossible). So substance is indivisible. Proposition 14 rounds out the discussion by explicitly affirming that God, the infinite, indivisible, necessarily existent substance is unique – other than God no substance can be or be conceived.

God as first cause of all (Part 1, Propositions 15–35)

God, the one substance, is the sole reality, according to Spinoza. This does not mean that there are no tables and chairs and trees and birds, clouds and candles, but it does mean that each of these individual everyday things must somehow be understood as a part, a product and a manifestation of the one divine substance. In order to understand this relationship between God and the things of this world we need to know more about God and about the way things follow from the power of God. In the remainder of Part 1 of the *Ethics* Spinoza tries to clarify these things and to prevent misunderstandings regarding this central point.

Proposition 15 and Scholium

Proposition 15 tells us that 'Whatever is, is in God, and nothing can be or be conceived without God.' Since God is all-inclusive, it comes as no surprise to learn that everything is in God. But for Spinoza, to say that something is 'in' God is not just to make a claim about the thing's location. On the contrary, as we noted above, it is to make a claim about ontological dependence and ultimately about causation.

The first part of the proposition states that everything that exists is ontologically dependent upon God and is caused by God. When first considering this concept, we used the example of a smile which is ontologically dependent upon a face. Without the face there could be no smile. But more than that – the smile has no real independent existence at all. It is just a certain way in which the features of the face can be configured. This is a fairly good analogy to the way Spinoza understands the relationship between God and individual things. Things are entirely dependent upon God; things are nothing but certain finite ways the divine substance is configured.

Spinoza sometimes uses the word 'thing' in this context, but he prefers the more technical term 'mode'. This term is defined in direct contrast to 'substance'. Substance is 'in itself and conceived through itself', while a mode is 'in another through which it is also conceived'. It is helpful to remember that the Latin term 'modus', which we translate as 'mode', originally just meant 'manner' or 'way' (as in *modus vivendi* – a way of living). A mode is just a certain way in which the features of the divine substance are configured.

Consider some physical object (which Spinoza would refer to as an 'extended mode' or a 'mode of extension') – say, a tree. As we saw above, extension is an attribute and is conceptually ultimate. Individual extended things are 'in' extension, but extension itself is not 'in' anything else. The tree is 'in' extension, and in order to conceptualize the tree we must think of it as a mode of extension – as a way in which the features of extension are configured. We must also think of it as being caused by extension.

It sounds a little odd to say that individual extended things are caused by extension, but it makes more sense if we remember that extension, as an attribute, is a way that we perceive the essence of God. God – cause of himself and of all that is – is powerful. Indeed, God/substance is power – power that expresses itself in an active way as the world around us. (In Proposition 34 Spinoza will explicitly equate God's essence and God's power.) There are (as we will learn later in the *Ethics*) uniform law-like regularities in accordance with which the power of God is expressed through the attribute of extension. Spinoza would call these the laws of extended nature (nowadays we would say the laws of physics), and everything that happens in the extended world happens in accordance with these laws – for the extended world, with all its blooming and buzzing richness, is nothing else than this power expressing itself in law-like ways. So to say that a certain extended mode, such as the tree, is caused by extension, is to say that the mode results from, and is a manifestation of, the power of God as expressed through the law-like workings of extended nature.

Spinoza pauses after Proposition 15 to insert a long Scholium on the subject of God and extension. He notes that some uneducated people tend to think of God in anthropomorphic terms, as if God had a body like ours, with arms and legs. Spinoza dismisses that view as absurd. But he knows that more sophisticated thinkers have thought of God as a purely spiritual being, and have denied any physicality or extended nature to God. Since Spinoza holds that extension is one of God's infinite attributes, revealing God's essence and power, he takes time to address those arguments with which previous theologians had sought to deny any extended character to God (1p15sch). The details of these arguments are not crucial to understanding Spinoza's views, but it is noteworthy that he draws an important distinction between the way we imagine things and the way we conceive them with the intellect. This will be important going forward.

Study question

1. What does Spinoza mean when he says that a mode cannot 'be or be conceived' without the substance of which it is a mode?

Propositions 16 and 17

Proposition 16 reiterates the importance of the fact that God is infinite, but combines that with mention of another crucial aspect of God's nature – its necessity. 'From the necessity of the divine nature there must follow infinitely many things in infinitely many modes [ways] . . .' Spinoza says that things 'follow from' the divine nature – a locution that reminds us that he thinks of this in quasi-logical or perhaps geometrical terms – things follow from the divine nature in something like the way a conclusion follows from the premises of an argument or geometrical truths follow from the definitions and axioms of geometry. The demonstration reinforces this impression, for we are told that from the definition of something the intellect infers certain properties that follow from the essence of that thing. The essence of God is infinite structured power, and from this power follow infinitely many things in infinitely many modes or ways. But note that Spinoza does not say that from God's nature these things *will* follow or that they *do* follow. He says that from the *necessity* of God's nature they *must* follow. This too is in keeping with the analogy of logical implication, for of course in a valid deductive argument the conclusion follows necessarily from the premises. But the emphasis on necessity introduces a central theme in Spinoza's philosophy that will be very important in the remainder of Part 1 and will re-emerge at central points throughout the rest of the *Ethics* as well.

Spinoza believes that he has demonstrated that the nature of God is necessarily as it is and that everything that exists follows necessarily from that nature in accordance with the laws of that nature. Since God is the absolute first cause, and since there is nothing outside of God that could cause God to do anything, Spinoza concludes, in Proposition 17, that 'God acts from the laws of his nature alone, and is compelled by no one.' The wording is a little misleading here, for when we read 'God acts ...' we naturally think of a person-like God, making up his mind to do something, and then acting. But Spinoza emphatically does not mean that God 'acts' in that sense. To say that God acts, in Spinoza's terminology, is just to say that things follow from the structured power which is the divine nature. To use Spinoza's favourite example: it follows from the nature of a triangle that its angles add up to 180 degrees. Odd though it sounds, Spinoza might say that the triangle 'acted', in that something followed from its nature. So, too, when everything that exists follows from the structured power which is the divine nature, God's nature is causing things to be as they are and to happen as they do – and thus God is (in Spinoza's sense) *acting*. And since God is not being induced or compelled by anything else to act as he does (remember: there is nothing else), the way God acts can only be following from his own nature – and the laws that are a part of that nature.

Spinoza concludes, in a corollary to Proposition 17, that God is a free cause – indeed that God is the only truly free cause. Spinoza is employing the definition of 'free' that he offered at the beginning of Part 1 (Definition 7), and his claim that God is a free cause makes good sense in light of that definition. 'That thing is called free which exists from the necessity of its nature alone, and is determined to act by itself alone ...' The claim that God exists by virtue of his own nature is familiar by now (Proposition 7), and there exists nothing by which God might be determined to act other than the divine nature itself. So God clearly fulfils the criteria for freedom stated in the definition.

But Spinoza knows that some readers will find it odd that immediately after demonstrating that God's nature is necessarily as it is and that all things *must* follow – *necessarily* – he claims that God is entirely free. How can all this necessity be compatible with freedom? Freedom is often thought to involve the power and the opportunity to choose between alternatives, but Spinoza's God makes no choices at all – things follow necessarily from the divine nature, with no choice involved. In the Scholium to Proposition 17, Spinoza tries to answer this sort of objection with regard to God's freedom, and in doing so he begins to lay the groundwork for his own positive account of human freedom – an account that is central to the later ethical parts of this work.

As is often the case, Spinoza uses the Scholium as an opportunity to argue more informally with those who hold views different from his own. He first addresses those who think that divine freedom entails that God has a choice – i.e. that he be able to do or not do that which is in his power.

> Others think that God is a free cause because he can (so they think) bring it about that the things we have said follow from his nature (i.e. which are in his power) do not happen or are not produced by him. But this is the same as if they were to say that God can bring it about that it would not follow from the nature of a triangle that its three angles are equal to two right angles ... – which is absurd. (1p17s)

Spinoza is attacking his opponents' conception of freedom by pointing out that in order for God to be free, according to their definition God would have to be able to act in a way that contradicts his own nature. But (Spinoza emphasizes) self-contradiction is not freedom; it is absurdity. It is as if one were to say that God is not free unless he can create a round square. But Spinoza thinks that to talk of round squares is not to talk of freedom, but to mouth unintelligible nonsense. So, too, to speak of even the possibility of something happening that is contrary to that which follows from God's nature is just absurd.

Spinoza wants to stake out his own position without engaging in endless debate, but he knows that there are deep issues lurking on all sides of this discussion. For example, Descartes seems to have held that the very laws of logic are true because God exercised his free will and mandated that they be so. Spinoza rejects that view entirely. By maintaining that God has a defined nature from which things follow necessarily, Spinoza is implicitly denying that God has a 'free will' at all. He knows that many thinkers have attributed such a will to God, for they have thought that this free will is the highest perfection in us, and so they naturally thought that God would have such a perfection in the highest degree. Then, having assigned a will to God, theologians argue about which is more basic to God's nature – His intellect or His will. Spinoza thinks that these controversies betray a complete misunderstanding of the divine nature. They show that the thinkers have confused human nature with the divine nature. They imagine God as thinking of things in his intellect and then bringing them about by an act of will. As Spinoza sees it, neither intellect nor will (as we understand these terms in application to ourselves) can be said to apply to God. On the contrary, if we do attribute will and intellect to God, we must understand these terms in a sense quite different from the way we understand them in reference to human beings. We will hear more about the problems with the notion of 'God's will' in the Appendix to Part 1.

Study questions

1. Spinoza's definition of freedom makes it possible for him to say that God acts absolutely necessarily and yet absolutely freely. How does his definition make it possible for necessity and freedom to be reconciled?
2. Does Spinoza's definition of freedom – in terms of being determined to act by oneself alone – capture what we normally mean by freedom?

Proposition 18

It has been established that God is the first cause of all that exists, but there remains a lot of unclarity about just how things 'follow from' the structured power that is the divine nature. Propositions 18–25 are intended to provide some clarification on this question. The first of these (18) explains that God is not the transient, but the immanent cause of things. These are terms that we no longer use these days, but their meaning is clear enough. Were God the transient cause of things, he would bring them about, the causation would cease, and they would then exist separate from and independent of the divine causal impulse. To say that God is the immanent cause is to say that things are produced in God by God, and that they remain in God as the divine power that produced them remains in them. Our example is overly simple, but we can again think of the smile that is a configuration of the features of the face. The facial features that cause the smile remain immanent in the smile as the smile remains in the face.

Propositions 21–23
Knowing that as an immanent cause God remains present in the effect does not, by itself, clarify the causal process very much. Unfortunately Spinoza never does make it entirely clear. But he provides some help in understanding the process when he distinguishes between those things that follow from the absolute nature of God's attributes and those that follow in a more indirect or derivative way. The former (we are told in Proposition 21) are infinite and must have always existed. This is not surprising, for the attribute itself expresses the essence of God, which is infinite and timeless. Those things that follow directly from the absolute nature of the attribute could be expected to inherit these characteristics of the attributes and hence themselves be eternal and infinite.

These things (if 'things' is the right word) are usually referred to in the scholarly literature as the 'immediate infinite and eternal modes'. But there is not much agreement about exactly what Spinoza is talking about here. Propositions 21–23 (in which this doctrine is presented in the *Ethics*) are quite abstract and give us very little to go on. The demonstration of Proposition 21 is especially opaque, even by Spinoza's standards. Fortunately Spinoza has addressed this issue in a couple of other places in his writings. In order to grasp even the general outline of his view we would do well to consult what he has to say in these other passages.

Spinoza was asked by an astute correspondent (Tschirnhaus) about this doctrine, and he responded (Letter 64) with more detail than in the *Ethics*. Under the attribute of thought, he says, the immediate infinite mode is 'absolutely infinite intellect'. This is not entirely clear, but we can put it together with the fact that for Spinoza the intellect consists of ideas – of (so to speak) thinkings of things. (There will be more on this subject when we get to Part 2 of the *Ethics*.) On this reading, the absolutely infinite intellect consists of the infinite ideas of everything that there is. Even this is somewhat ambiguous, though. Is it an infinitely large collection of ideas or is it a collection of ideas that are infinite because they are universally applicable to an infinity of things (and perhaps generative of an infinity of further ideas)? In either case the attribute is a boundless structured power of thinking, and from its absolute nature follow infinite ideas of all there is. Since that power is eternal and since the 'following' is the timeless 'following' of logical implication, there is no place for the introduction of temporal considerations here – no more than in geometry itself.

Switching from the attribute of thought to the attribute of extension (the one other attribute known to us), Spinoza tells Tschirnhaus that the immediate infinite mode is 'motion and rest'. How shall we understand this? It might mean just that a universal truth about extended things – a truth that follows from the very nature of extension – is that extended things are capable of moving or of being at rest. But that interpretation hardly seems to do justice to the fact that the attribute of extension reflects the infinite structured power of God or substance. Perhaps the claim is that the power that is extension is immediately expressed as an infinity of things in motion and at rest. That suggestion goes in the right direction, but (as we will see) Spinoza thinks that more levels of mediation and interaction are required before an infinite series of individual things in motion is produced.

In trying to understand the infinite and eternal modes that follow immediately from the absolute nature of the attribute (i.e. in trying to understand Propositions 21–23), we would do well to remember that a mode is a manner or way in which the power of God/substance is expressed as activity. An infinite and eternal mode of extension is then a timeless way in which the power of God is expressed throughout the boundless extended realm. When Spinoza suggests 'motion and rest' as a title for that mode, we can think of it as a way in which motion and rest occur always and everywhere throughout extended nature.

A very plausible interpretation of this kind has been suggested by E. M. Curley.[4] Curley recommends that we think of the infinite modes along the lines of the laws of nature. They are law-like ways in which physical nature always and everywhere acts. They can rightly be thought of as eternal, for, like the truths of geometry, they make no reference to time and are not subject to change in the course of time. All things happen and change in accordance with these laws, but the laws themselves do not change. On this reading, when Spinoza speaks of 'motion and rest' as the immediate infinite and eternal mode under the attribute of extension, the term 'motion and rest' is a stand-in for the most general laws of physical nature – or, to be precise, the most general ways in which God/substance, understood through the attribute of extension, always and everywhere acts. From these most universal and fundamental laws follow other laws of nature, likewise unlimited in application, that will jointly determine the overall structural features and composition of the whole universe and will govern the interactions among finite extended things in the world. In fact, in the letter to Tschirnhaus Spinoza refers to this next-level mediate infinite and eternal mode as the 'face (or make) of the whole universe'.

Propositions 24–27

Thus far we have learned of those modes which follow from the absolute nature of God and thereby inherit the timelessness and infinity that is characteristic of the divine nature. Spinoza seems concerned that the reader might gain the false impression that these infinite and eternal modes have acquired a kind of independent ontological status of their own. Propositions 24–27 are intended to counter that impression. Proposition 24 reminds us that the essence of things produced by God does not involve existence. Even the infinite and eternal modes that we have been discussing, which do indeed exist eternally, do so not in virtue of their own essence or power, but in virtue of the power of God from which they follow with timeless necessity. If the essence of these modes did involve existence, they would be 'in themselves' – they would require nothing else in order to exist – i.e. they would not be modes at all, but substances. The corollary to Proposition 25 reminds us that 'Particular things are nothing but ... modes by which God's attributes are expressed in a certain and determinate way.'

Proposition 26 reminds us that whatever characteristics, and also whatever causal powers a things might have, follow from God. 'A thing which has been determined to produce an effect has necessarily been determined in this way by God; and one which has not been determined by God cannot determine itself to produce an effect.' In the following proposition Spinoza makes it clear that a mode cannot, as it were, resist the power of God by failing or refusing to do that which it is causally determined to do. 'A thing which has been determined by God to produce an effect, cannot render itself undetermined.'

Proposition 28

Until this point Spinoza has focused on those things which, because they follow from the absolute nature of God, must be infinite and eternal. Now he is finally ready to address the question of finite modes – 'those singular things which are finite and have a determinate existence'. The first thing to note about the discussion is that Spinoza does not try to prove that such finite things exist. Perhaps he thinks that he has already done that in Proposition 16. In any case, at this point he seems to take it as a given that there are such finite determinate things, and he seeks to explain the way in which they follow from the infinite structured power of God. We know, from Propositions 21 and 22, that these things cannot follow from the absolute nature of an attribute, for if they did they would be infinite and eternal. Spinoza claims that they must therefore be determined to exist and to act by another finite thing. That other finite thing must, in turn, be determined to exist and to act by yet another finite thing, and so on ad infinitum. This suggests an infinite series of finite things, in which each one affects the next-in-line – helping to bring it into existence and conditioning the ways in which it acts.

So – there are infinite and eternal modes that follow from the absolute nature of God, and there is an infinite series of finite things that have a determinate existence. How are these two types of modes related to each other, and how does each play a role in the production of reality as we know it? Here again a reading based on Curley's interpretation is very helpful. According to this reading the infinite and eternal modes are omnipresent nomological regularities of the workings of nature – law-like ways in which God/nature always and everywhere acts. These regularities are universal, so they cannot, by themselves, bring about any singular finite things. But given their law-like character they can govern the interactions among singular things. To take a simple example of the sort that is often used in discussions of causation, consider a billiard ball (say, the eight ball) in motion across the table. This moving billiard ball is a finite mode of extension. By virtue of its motion it is capable of setting other balls in motion as well. Spinoza suggests that this billiard ball must have been set in motion by another (say, the cue ball). But what effect the cue ball's colliding with the eight ball will have is a matter of the laws of nature (specifically the laws of impact, momentum, etc.). So in order for that finite and determinate mode (the moving eight ball) to be brought about, it must be determined to be and to act by another finite mode (i.e. the eight ball must be hit by another ball) and the infinite and eternal modes must play a role as well (there must be law-like regularities that govern what happens when one rolling spherical object collides with a stationary spherical object of similar mass).

In discussing this point scholars have often spoken of 'the two causal series' at work in Spinoza's theory – the vertical and the horizontal orders of causation. The vertical order begins with the attribute. From the structured power that is the attribute (say, extension) follow certain law-like ways in which the power of God/ nature is always and everywhere expressed. Those regularities then condition and govern the interactions of the endless series of finite things that constitute the horizontal causal order. Both are required in order to produce the infinite variety of things that follow from the divine nature.

Study questions

1. How do the vertical and horizontal orders of causation differ from each other? How do they both contribute to the production of finite modes?

Propositions 29–33 – Determinism and necessity

It has been clear all along – or at least since Proposition 16 and the Scholium to 17 (see p. 31) – that necessity pervades the Spinozistic system. God necessarily exists and necessarily has the nature that he has. Everything that exists follows necessarily from that divine nature. Every mode is determined to be and to act as it does – conditioned by other modes in accordance with the regular ways in which God necessarily always and everywhere acts. Spinoza has left little room for doubt in this regard, and yet at the end of Part 1 he devotes a series of propositions to the task of repeating and re-emphasizing this central point.

Why does he proceed in this way? It seems that having completed the outline of his account of how all things are in God and follow from God, Spinoza wants to fill in a gap or two and to ward off a couple of misunderstandings that might make it difficult for readers to grasp his position. First he reiterates, with great clarity, the thesis of universal causal determinism: 'In nature there is nothing contingent, but all things have been determined from the necessity of the divine nature to exist and to produce an effect in a certain way' (Proposition 29). But Spinoza thinks that it will be hard for people to accept this so long as they continue to hold a more traditional conception of God and the creation of the world. Since he has spoken of the power of God and of that power expressing itself, perhaps he fears that some will continue to think in terms of God choosing to exercise his power by an act of divine will.

To ward off this misunderstanding Spinoza introduces a distinction of his own to differentiate the active power of God from its expression as the world. He will then argue that if there were anything like a divine will, it would be on the latter side of this divide – i.e. it would be a product of the divine creative activity rather than an active power responsible for making that process happen. He hopes thereby to put a further nail into the coffin of the misleading idea that God, in an exercise of will, chose to create the world.

Spinoza's own distinction is drawn in the Scholium to Proposition 29 where he speaks of the distinction between *natura naturans* and *natura naturata*. *Natura naturans* ('nature naturing' in English) refers to the active aspect of God – i.e. the divine power that, in expressing itself as activity, produces the world. The self-expression of that power, seen as a series of modes in interaction with each other, is *natura naturata* ('nature natured'). It is important to be clear that these are not two different realities. Rather, they are two ways of conceptualizing one reality.

An analogy might be helpful here (though it is only an analogy). We can think of God's activity along the lines of a dance. Dancing can be viewed as a structured activity, and can also be referred to as a thing, by use of a noun – 'a dance'. The thing is both the result of the activity and, in an important sense, identical with the activity. Furthermore, if we know something about the structure of a particular dance (say, a waltz or a merengue) we can infer various movements and configurations of the dancer's body at various stages of the dance. This analogy is helpful in clarifying how one thing could be both activity (dancing) and thing (a dance) – depending on how it is viewed. But it must be used with care, for it is also misleading, since dancing presupposes an independent agent who is doing the dancing, whereas God is not separable (except conceptually) from the divine activity.

Having distinguished the active from the passive or the producing from the produced (so to speak), Spinoza argues, in Proposition 31, that specific thoughts and volitions (whether in God or in us) are modes of the attribute of thinking and must be ascribed to the 'produced' side of things – i.e. to *natura naturata*. It is thus obvious that these thoughts and volitions are determined to be what they are by the active power that produced them. The will consists of individual volitions (according to Spinoza), and each of these volitions is a finite mode, determined to be what it is by other finite modes and by the laws of the attribute of thought. Since they are in this way determined by other things, they cannot be considered free. Thus Spinoza concludes that 'The will cannot be called a free cause, but only a necessary one' (1p32). Having thus denied that any free will is possible, he promptly infers, as a corollary, that God does not produce anything by means of free will.

The final assertion of Spinoza's uncompromisingly deterministic position comes in Proposition 33 where we read that 'Things could have been produced by God in no other way, and in no other order than they have been produced.' In defending this claim Spinoza argues that since all things follow from the nature of God, if it were possible for things to have been produced in another way, it would have to be possible for God to have had a different nature. But since he has proved that the divine nature is singular and unique, he concludes that God could not have had a different nature, and hence that nothing could have been different from the way it actually is.

Spinoza knows that this view (that God could not have created things differently) is not a widely held or a positively regarded view in most quarters. In his own day most people accepted the biblical account of creation – an account that Spinoza rejects as an anthropomorphic figment of an ancient writer's imagination. But also more thoughtful and philosophically sophisticated thinkers had held, as a central tenet of their doctrines, that God could have produced a different world. Descartes, as we noted above, held that God created everything by an act of his radically free and unconstrained will. According to this view God could have made it the case that even the laws of logic or mathematics were different if he had so chosen. Spinoza sees this as (literally) unthinkable. Leibniz, a younger contemporary of Spinoza, developed an elaborate view according to which God chose among a number of possible worlds – 'possible' in the sense that they were internally consistent and coherent, and that any one of them could have come into being had God chosen to actualize it. According to Leibniz, though any of these could have been chosen, it was certain that God, in his divine perfection, would in fact choose to actualize the best of these possible worlds. But in spite of the fact that God's choice of the best was a foregone conclusion, Leibniz nonetheless insisted that the other worlds were possible and that they could have been actualized. Spinoza rejects this view, as well, for it assumes that there is a standard of goodness, independent of and prior to God, to which God looks in deciding what to do. But there is of course nothing independent of and prior to God.

Spinoza holds that all of these views are misguided, and that they ultimately derive from an erroneous conception of the nature of God and of his creative activity. So long as we think of God as having human-like psychological characteristics – i.e. so long as we think of God as making choices and decisions, we will mistakenly imagine that the world might have been different from the way it is. Only when we realize that the divine nature is what it must be, given that it is substance, and that the world follows from the divine nature 'with the same necessity as it follows from the nature of a triangle that its angles total 180 degrees' will we rightly understand God. And only then, Spinoza would add, will we be in a position to understand ourselves and the world.

Appendix

The basic account of God/substance/nature is complete. But Spinoza knows that the view he is espousing is unusual and difficult, and that it is an uphill struggle to get his readers to understand and to accept his position. After completing the geometrical exposition he takes the unusual step of setting the formal apparatus aside and addressing the reader in a more accessible (almost conversational) way. He starts with an excellent brief summary of the contents of Part 1:

> With these [demonstrations] I have explained God's nature and properties: that he exists necessarily; that he is unique; that he is and acts from the necessity alone of his nature; that (and how) he is the free cause of all things; that all things are in God and so depend on him that without him they can neither be nor be conceived; and finally that all things have been predetermined by

READING THE TEXT

God, not from freedom of the will or absolute good pleasure, but from God's absolute nature or infinite power.

Spinoza thinks that his readers will have difficulty appreciating and accepting this view because of certain prejudices that block their understanding. In the remainder of the Appendix he undertakes to bring these prejudices to light and to 'submit them to the scrutiny of reason'.

At the root of all of these prejudices is the fact that we tend to explain and understand things in terms of the ends which they serve. When human beings do things, they generally do them in order to achieve some end – some desire that they want to satisfy or some purpose that they have in mind. To explain and understand a human being's actions, then, we consider the agent's desires and purposes. To understand some human artefact or product (a table, a carriage, a house), we invoke the end or purpose served by the artefact. Spinoza does not object to this, of course, but he notes that there are serious problems caused by the fact that we tend to concentrate on this kind of explanation. For one thing, this kind of explanation is inherently deficient as an explanation; for another, all kinds of confusion arise when we apply this kind of explanation to non-human things in nature.

Regarding the first of these problems, Spinoza notes that we human beings naturally desire what is advantageous for us, and that we are consciously aware of these desires. According to Spinoza, these desires are part of the natural order and hence are caused by prior events and factors in accordance with the laws of nature. But we are unaware of the causes of our desires – indeed, people are generally unaware that their desires have any causes at all. So, when we want to explain something that a human being does, or some human artefact, we appeal to the agent's desires or purposes, and do not ask about the causes of those desires or purposes. And since we do not know about those causes, we tend to assume that there are no such causes, and we just attribute the desire, purpose or the action to the agent's 'free will' – allowing ourselves to be satisfied with that. But Spinoza thinks that this is an entirely unsatisfactory explanation. Indeed, it is no explanation at all, and yields no real knowledge or understanding. For Spinoza (we remember) it is axiomatic that 'The knowledge of an effect depends on and involves the knowledge of its cause.'

The other problem with our tendency to explain things in terms of ends, desires and purposes (what are sometimes called 'final causes') is that we mistakenly apply this kind of explanation to other things in nature. People find things that serve their needs – such as teeth for chewing, eyes for seeing, the sun for light – and they judge that these things exist *in order to* serve our needs and purposes. Since they know that they did not make these things themselves, they assume that someone else provided them for their use. And so they infer that, '... there was a ruler, or number of rulers of nature, endowed with human freedom, who had taken care of all things for them, and made all things for their use.' Then they seek out ways to worship and to ingratiate themselves to this ruler, '... so that God might love them above all the rest, and direct the whole of nature according to the needs of their blind desire and insatiable greed'. And when damaging things happen (such as storms, diseases, etc.) they judge that these are the result of God's being angry with them. When they notice that often good people suffer and the unjust prosper, they declare the ways of God inscrutable '... and so remain in the state of ignorance in which they had been born'.

Spinoza thinks that the attempt to understand things in nature in terms of ends and purposes leads us astray. Natural events do not happen in order to fulfil some purpose. They happen because they are caused to happen by prior causes in accordance with the laws of nature – laws that make no mention of ends or purposes at all. Besides, to say that God acts in order to achieve some purpose or to fulfil some desire of his is to say that God lacks something and desires it. But an infinite being cannot lack anything.

This kind of thinking – i.e. the attempt to understand things in terms of ends and in terms of God's purposes – is a dead end. Eventually these explanations end in the claim that it is God's will that it be so. Spinoza says of people who invoke the will of God in this way, that they have taken '... refuge in the will of God, i.e., the sanctuary of ignorance'. He also maintains (in a salute to his own century) that this tendency to invoke the inscrutable will of God '... would have caused the truth to be hidden from the human race to eternity, if Mathematics, which is concerned not with ends, but only with the essences and properties of figures, had not shown man another standard of truth'.

In some of the sharpest language that Spinoza uses in the *Ethics*, he takes to task those who, instead of seeking the natural causes of unusual events, attribute them to supernatural intervention and call them miracles. If a miracle is supposed to be an event that contravenes the laws of nature, then Spinoza does not believe that there are or ever have been any miracles. He notes that once an event has been deemed a miracle, no further effort is made to arrive at a natural explanation for it. Those who do continue looking for natural explanations of putatively miraculous events are looked down upon by the faithful. '... [O]ne who seeks the true causes of miracles and is eager, like an educated man, to understand natural things, not to wonder at them like a fool, is generally considered and denounced as an impious heretic by those whom the people honor as interpreters of nature and the Gods.' Spinoza even takes a swipe at those clerics who maintain their power by keeping the people in ignorance and awe.

In a final set of arguments near the end of the Appendix, Spinoza points out a further consequence of the tendency to think that things happen in order to be of service to us. We tend to think that the most important characteristics that things have are the ones that make the greatest impression on us. We come up with notions that reflect the ways in which we are affected by things that we experience, and we erroneously think that these notions reflect characteristics of the things themselves. Spinoza specifically mentions good and evil, order and confusion, warmth and cold, beauty and ugliness. Each of these, he thinks, really describes something about the way in which we are affected by things (rather than something about the things themselves). As we will soon learn in Part 2, Spinoza uses the term 'imagination' to refer not only to what we today would call imagination, but also to our sensory experience. (This was a common usage in his time – a result, in part, of the fact that we form 'images' of things when we perceive them with the senses.) Spinoza thinks that the aforementioned characteristics (good, evil, beauty, ugliness, etc.) refer to the way our imaginations are affected by things, and hence he calls them 'beings of imagination' (*entia imaginationis*). For example, '... if the motion the nerves receive from objects presented through the eyes is conducive to health, the objects by which it is caused are called beautiful; those which cause a contrary motion are called ugly'. The point is that we think of beauty and ugliness as properties of the things in the world, but in fact they are characteristics of the way the things affect our senses.

On the whole, people are quite similar to each other in their make-up and constitution. But there are of course differences as well. Since these notions of good and evil, beauty and ugliness, etc. refer to the ways our senses are affected by things that we perceive, different individuals with slightly different constitutions often differ in their judgments regarding these notions. This leads to disagreement and discord, and eventually (since no agreement can be reached) to scepticism. Spinoza thinks that this kind of disagreement and scepticism can be overcome only via mathematics and the new sciences of nature, for these are focused on the real and essential properties of things, not the ways in which things affect our deceptive senses.

This differentiation between the properties that things really do have and those that actually exist only in the observer was very important in Spinoza's day. Galileo had drawn the distinction quite clearly in a work entitled *The Assayer*, and the point was accepted by Descartes and others as well. The two groups of properties came to be known as 'primary' and 'secondary' properties, and despite extensive criticism over the centuries (by Bishop Berkeley, for example), the distinction is still widely accepted and employed today. The doctrine will play an especially important role in Spinoza's theory, as we will see in Part 2 of the *Ethics*.

PART 2 – ON THE NATURE AND ORIGIN OF THE MIND

Part 1 has provided the basic metaphysical concepts that structure the account of reality. As he makes the transition into Part 2 Spinoza reminds the reader that there is an ethical motivation for all this theorizing.

> I pass now to explaining those things which must necessarily follow from the essence of God, or the infinite and eternal Being – not, indeed, all of them, for we have demonstrated (1p16) that infinitely many things must follow from it in infinitely many modes, but only those that can lead us, by the hand as it were, to the knowledge of the human mind and its highest blessedness.

Why does the focus turn immediately to the human mind? The main reason is that as an ethicist Spinoza wants to understand human happiness and 'blessedness', and happiness and contentment are states of *mind*. In addition, Spinoza thinks that among the chief causes of our unhappiness are certain false beliefs that we hold. In order to learn the truth and thereby get rid of these erroneous beliefs, it would help to know how we acquire knowledge and why we so often fall into error. But such knowledge of how human cognition works (and fails to work) requires knowledge of the mind. Part 2 of the *Ethics* is intended to provide that knowledge.

In terms of content, we can divide up Part 2 into three sections. (1) The first section encompasses Propositions 1–13 and deals, in a systematic way, with the relationship between the attribute of extension and the attribute of thinking – between extended things and the ideas of extended things. The last three propositions (2p11–13) apply the general point to the human mind and body. (2) Having established that the mind is 'the idea of the body', Spinoza finds that in order to understand the mind he must delve more deeply into the nature of the human body as a finite mode of extension. This requires at least a sketch of basic physics. The second section of Part 2 provides that account in a series of lemmas inserted between Propositions 13 and 14. (3) The third section, Propositions 14–49, comprises the bulk of Part 2. In this section we learn about false ideas of the imagination (2p14–31, 35–36), true ideas of reason (2p32–34, 37–47) and the nature of the human will (2p48 & 49). The order in which Spinoza considers these questions is dictated by the subject matter itself. We will follow that order as well.

The context – Descartes and the mind–body problem

The most widely accepted modern view of the mind in the seventeenth century was that of Descartes. As we noted above (in Chapter 2) Descartes held that there are two types of created substance in this world – extended (i.e. physical) substance and mental substance. A human being's mind is an individual mental substance capable of thinking, doubting, loving, etc. Since this mind is also capable of determining itself to act, Descartes uses this theory to support our everyday belief in free will. This account squares in many ways with our common sense view of the mind, but it has a number of glaring problems.

One of the main problems is that it is difficult to explain how there can be interactions between two entirely different kinds of substances – one physical and the other utterly non-physical.

Occurrences in our bodies (say, appendicitis or a stubbed toe) can cause things to happen in our minds (experiences of pain). Conversely, thoughts in my mind (I want to get there more quickly) can cause changes in my physical body (an increase in my rate of walking). But how, on the Cartesian model, can there be this kind of causal interaction in either direction? Descartes hypothesized that there is in the brain a tiny, easily movable organ called the pineal gland. This gland is so sensitive that it can be moved by thoughts (such as the thought that I am in a hurry), even though thoughts are not physical at all. Having been moved by a thought, its motion can then set in motion a train of physical causes and effects that will result in my walking more quickly. Conversely, occurrences in my appendix can, through a chain of physical causes, set my pineal gland in motion, and this physical motion can somehow cause in me the mental event which is an experience of pain. With this theory, Descartes seeks to solve the problem of the interaction between the mind and the body – that is, between mental substance and physical substance. Spinoza had great admiration for Descartes, but he found this Cartesian theory entirely unconvincing. (He almost ridicules this Cartesian view later, in the Preface to Part 5 of the *Ethics*.)

Of course Spinoza had additional objections to Descartes' view – beyond the fact that the latter had no plausible explanation for the interaction of mind and body. Descartes held that the mind and the body are two different substances. But this is entirely unacceptable from Spinoza's point of view, for Spinoza has proven that there can be only one substance – the infinite and eternal God. And the human mind, in its volitional aspect, cannot be self-determining, for the human mind is a finite thing and every finite thing is determined by other finite things in accordance with the laws of nature. The Cartesian theory cannot be correct. But if the mind and the body are not substances, what are they?

Propositions 1–10 – Extended things and their ideas
There are few philosophical topics as old or as difficult as the mind–body problem. And there are few areas in which Spinoza's originality shows up as clearly as in the treatment of this question. His account of the nature of the mind is not accepted by today's theorists, but it is still read and consulted because it represents a genuinely novel approach to this old problem.

READING THE TEXT

Spinoza does not begin with the relationship between the human mind and the human body at all. He notes that there are thoughts or ideas, and, in accordance with his overall metaphysical system, outlined in Part 1, he holds thought to be an attribute of God, and sees individual thoughts or ideas as modes under this attribute – i.e. as specific ways in which the one power of thinking can be expressed (2p1). Likewise, he notes that there are extended things, and in line with his metaphysics, he sees extension as an attribute and sees individual extended things as modes under this attribute – i.e. as specific ways in which the one divine power acts extendedly in accordance with the laws of extension (2p2).

Since God's power of thinking (just like his power of acting extendedly) is infinite, there will be, in God, ideas of his essence (power) and indeed ideas of everything that follows from that essence (2p3). The ideas will follow from God's power of thinking just as the extended things follow from God's power of acting extendedly.

There is some controversy over just what an *idea* is for Spinoza. He repeatedly emphasizes that an idea is not a 'picture'. For him an idea is more like a proposition – not because it is inherently linguistic in character (on the contrary, Spinoza's ideas certainly do not consist of words), but because ideas, like propositions, assert that something is the case. It seems that for Spinoza an idea of a certain state of affairs would be a thinking-that-it-is-the-case. One commentator suggested that we think of an idea of something (in Spinoza's theory) as 'the truth about the thing'. We cannot enter into the details of this extensive debate, but the reader of the *Ethics* should be mindful that ideas are not dumb pictures, but rather active thinkings.

Spinoza emphasizes, in 2p5 and 2p6, that the extended things do not cause the ideas, nor do the ideas cause the extended things. On the contrary, the entire infinite series of ideas (modes of thought) is caused by the infinite power of God expressed through the attribute of thought. The entire infinite series of extended things (modes of extension) is caused by that same infinite power of God, expressed through the attribute of extension. The modes of each attribute are caused by God insofar as he is considered through the attribute of which they are modes.

This leads to one of the most important propositions in the *Ethics*: 'The order and connection (*ordo et connexio*) of ideas is the same as the order and connection of things' (2p7). The proof of this proposition is not very helpful at this stage (though if we look back at it after completing Part 2 it makes sense). It is pretty clear, though, why Spinoza thinks this proposition is true. God's power is a structured power, and things are caused by and follow from that structured power in an orderly way (in accordance with the vertical and horizontal causal orders that were discussed above – p. 39). If we conceive the whole series of modes caused by that power through the attribute of extension, we find an infinite series of extended things caused by and related to each other in a well-structured way. If we conceive the whole series of modes caused by that power through the attribute of thought, we find an infinite series of ideas or thoughts, caused by and related to each other in a well-structured way. It is the very same structured power that is expressed through both of these series of modes – the extended and the thinking. Thus it is no surprise that the order and connection of things would be the same as the order and connection of ideas.

The doctrine that Spinoza has arrived at (and that we will be exploring in much greater detail) is sometimes referred to as 'parallelism'. It is so called because we can conceive of the two causal series, the mental and the physical (i.e. the ordered series of modes under the attribute of thought and the ordered series of modes under the attribute of extension), as running parallel to each other, matched up at every point. For every idea there is an exactly corresponding mode of extension – Spinoza calls that corresponding mode of extension the *ideatum* of the idea. For every mode of extension – every physical object in the world – there is an exactly corresponding mode of thought. There is, for every extended thing, an idea of that thing.

We must pause for a moment at that phrase ('idea of an extended thing') in order to forestall possible confusion. At this point in the development of Spinoza's view the phrase 'idea of a thing' is ambiguous. On the one hand it means the idea or mode of thought in the series of ideas that is the correlate or counterpart of the extended thing (the *ideatum*) in the parallel series of extended things. But in ordinary usage, the phrase 'the idea of a thing' means an idea that is *about* the thing – i.e. the idea that has the thing as its intentional content. The idea of a specific maple tree (in *this* sense) is *about* that maple tree. Which of these meanings does Spinoza have in mind when he says that there is, for each extended thing, an idea of that thing?

READING THE TEXT

Spinoza means both. The idea of the tree is the idea that is the parallel ideational correlate of the physical object that is the tree. But, according to Spinoza this same idea of the tree is also *about* the tree – it has the tree as its intentional content. Part of what makes this seem odd is that the 'parallelism' model, while helpful in some ways, is also misleading in other ways. It suggests that we are dealing with two separate series of distinct things running parallel with one another. But in fact there is only one series of modes here, expressed in two ways (2p7sch). So the tree and the idea of the tree (like any *ideatum* and the idea of that *ideatum*) are not two different modes, but one mode conceived of through two different attributes. The tree is an extended mode; the idea of the tree is a mode of thought – it is a thinking (a thought, an idea) of the tree. These two are in fact one mode of substance, expressed in two ways.

Sometimes Spinoza speaks of all the modes of thought, taken together, as 'the divine intellect' or even 'the mind of God'. We must keep in mind that terms like 'the mind of God' refer to the infinite ordered series of modes under the attribute of thought – an order that corresponds exactly to (because it is substantially identical to) the order of modes under the attribute of extension. Note, by the way, that since there is an idea in the 'mind of God' of every mode of substance, Spinoza can affirm, in his idiosyncratic way, the traditional theological doctrine of God's omniscience.

Before proceeding, Spinoza devotes 2p8 to the effort to clear up a difficult and puzzling issue. It may have occurred to the reader that there are things which existed in the past (but no longer exist), and things which do not yet exist (but will do so in the future) of which there are nonetheless ideas. For example (and this is not Spinoza's example), dinosaurs once existed, though they do not exist now. It seems, though, as if there are ideas of dinosaurs, for people think and talk about dinosaurs. If there is a perfect parallelism, it would seem that if there are no dinosaurs at present there would be no ideas of dinosaurs at present.

In order to answer this difficulty fully, we would need the entire theory of the imagination – which we will not get to until later in Part 2. But Spinoza wants to say that there is a sense in which what he calls the 'formal essence' of something can be 'contained' in God's attributes even at those times when the thing itself does not exist. This is one of the few places in the *Ethics* where he tries to provide the reader with an example to clarify his point – but unfortunately his example (a geometrical example, as usual) does not help very much. The best way to understand what he has in mind here is to remember what was said earlier in this chapter about the law-like ways in which God always and everywhere acts – those regularities of God's active expression that we try to describe when we talk of the 'laws of nature'. The laws of nature are such that when the right causal conditions obtain, dinosaurs come into being. The laws of nature do not rule out the possibility of dinosaurs – on the contrary, they mandate the existence of dinosaurs when the right climatic, genetic, geological, etc. conditions are fulfilled. Spinoza's way of saying this is to say that the formal essences of dinosaurs are contained (timelessly) in the attribute of extension (even though, at this present moment in history, the causal conditions for the actual existence of dinosaurs are not being fulfilled). He then defends the parallelism by saying that the ideas of dinosaurs are likewise (timelessly) comprehended in the attribute of thought even at those times when there are no ideas of actually existing dinosaurs. In trying to understand this point, it is helpful to remember that the parallelism (which, remember, is really an identity) holds not only among the finite modes of the horizontal order of causation, but also among the infinite and eternal modes of the vertical order of causation. So, in the same way that the physical/causal possibility of dinosaurs follows from the law-like regularities of nature's workings, the idea thereof follows from the ideas of those regularities. The parallel (identity) holds up and down the vertical order of causation, just as it holds all along the horizontal order.

One rather technical point that was mentioned above in connection with 2p5 and 2p6 needs to be emphasized again. According to Spinoza, when we are providing a causal account of a mode of extension, we must explain that mode in terms of the laws of the attribute of extension (items in the vertical order of causation) and other finite modes in the horizontal order of extension. And when we are providing an account of a mode of thought (an idea) we must do so in terms of the laws of the attribute of thought (items in the vertical order of causation) and other finite modes (i.e. other ideas) in the horizontal order of thought. Even though we know that the order of extension and the order of thought are perfectly parallel – indeed, even though we know that every mode of extension is, as a mode of substance, identical with a mode of thought –

we are not permitted to explain thoughts by reference to extended things or to explain extended things by reference to thoughts. For purposes of our conception and our understanding, these are two separate and self-contained causal orders.

2p9 presents a reprise of 1p28, but with an emphasis on ideas. An idea of a finite existing thing (which is itself, of course, a finite existing idea) cannot follow from God insofar as he is infinite, but only insofar as he is considered to be affected by the idea of another finite existing thing, etc. This is no surprise, of course, for the parallelism/identity guarantees that everything we said earlier about a moving billiard ball (in our discussion of 1p28) would be true (*mutatis mutandis*) of the idea of a moving billiard ball. The corollary to this proposition draws out, however, an important implication. If something happens in an extended mode, the idea of it will be in God only insofar as the idea of the extended mode is in God. Again, this follows from 2p7 – from the fact that the order and connection of ideas is the same as the order and connection of things.

Spinoza pauses at 2p10 to remind us that 'the being of substance does not pertain to the essence of man'. This seems to mean that although it follows from the nature of God that there can be such things as human beings – that indeed there will be human beings if and when certain causal conditions are fulfilled – still, necessary existence is not a characteristic of our human nature or of any of us as individual human beings. Spinoza appeals to the first Axiom of Part 2, which states that 'The essence of man does not involve necessary existence, i.e. from the order of nature it can happen equally that this or that man does exist, or that he doesn't exist.'

There is a danger of confusion here. It might sound as if Spinoza is claiming that it is not determined, one way or the other, whether a specific individual man exists or not. But he made it crystal clear earlier (1p33 & sch) that absolutely everything is causally determined to be exactly as it is. Is he contradicting himself? No, in this case, the inconsistency is only apparent. Whether a given man exists or not is absolutely and completely determined by the causal orders as they follow from God. So if a man exists, he exists necessarily. But the necessity here is not to be found in man's nature or essence. Man's existence does not follow from his essence or nature (after all, if it did, he would be God). The necessity with which we exist is a derivative necessity – derived from the nature and essence of God.

Study questions

1. In what sense are the modes under the attribute of thought identical with the modes under the attribute of extension?
2. Why is the relationship between ideas and extended modes sometimes called a 'parallelism'?
3. In what sense can Spinoza claim that his views affirm the traditional doctrine that God is omniscient?
4. What does it mean to say that the formal essences of things are included in God's attributes even if, at some specific time, the things themselves do not exist?

Propositions 11–13 – The mind as the idea of the body

In 2p11 Spinoza is prepared to establish what the human mind is. Since there exists nothing but substance and the modes under the attributes, the mind, characterized by thinking, must consist of modes of the attribute of thinking – i.e. ideas. By a process of elimination Spinoza establishes that the *ideatum* of the idea that is the human mind must be an actually existing finite thing. It cannot, after all, be the idea of an infinite thing, for if it were, it would be infinite and it would always exist by the necessity of its own nature. (And this is absurd, by 2a1.) But it also cannot be the idea of something that does not exist (or the idea would not actually exist). So it must be the idea of an actually existing finite thing. As we will learn in 2p13, it is the idea of the actually existing human body.

In the first sentence of the corollary to 2p11 Spinoza states that 'From this it follows that the human Mind is a part of the infinite intellect of God.' This is an extraordinary claim, though if we remember that what he calls here the infinite intellect of God is the series of modes under the attribute of thought, it seems a little less strange. Still, Spinoza knows that this whole account of the human mind will strike many readers as simply incredible. So in the Scholium to 2p11 he warns us to take it slowly and suspend our judgement until we have read through the entire theory.

The rest of 2p11c presents an extremely important doctrine, but its central significance for the *Ethics* is not apparent until later in Part 2, where Spinoza discusses how we human beings go wrong in our thinking. We will postpone our detailed consideration of this passage (2p11c) until then (see pp. 69–71 below).

Proposition 12 introduces a turn of phrase that will be important for Spinoza's account of human sense-perception and our acquisition of knowledge. 'Whatever happens in the object of the idea constituting the human mind must be perceived by the human mind, *or* there will necessarily be an idea of that thing in the mind; i.e., if the object of the idea constituting a human mind is a body, nothing can happen in that body which is not perceived by the mind.' It is easy to understand why Spinoza holds that there will be an idea in the mind of everything that happens in the body that is the object of the mind. The parallelism (2p7) guarantees that (though there might be some question about what the term 'in' means with reference to an idea being 'in' the mind). But note how he moves from 'there will be an idea of it in the mind' to 'it must be perceived by the mind'. This will be fundamental in Spinoza's account of perception and knowledge. The presence of the idea of something in the mind is tantamount to the mind's perceiving that something.

The attentive reader of the text will note that 2p12 seems to entail that I will 'perceive' everything that happens in my body. Does this mean that I will consciously be aware of changes in my blood pressure or the growth of the hair on my head? Let us hope that it does not mean this, for quite obviously I am not aware of these things that are happening in my body. A general principle of charitable interpretation should keep us from interpreting an author in such a way as to attribute patently false claims to him or her – unless there is no alternative interpretation available. We will return to this question when we have more of Spinoza's account of perception in hand – to see if we can plausibly avoid having to attribute this implausible claim to him.

2p13 finally clearly embraces the doctrine that Spinoza has been leading up to – the mind is an idea and the object (*ideatum*) of that idea is the body. The demonstration of this proposition is based on the straightforward experiential fact that I feel it when things happen to my body. This seems so obvious and fundamental to Spinoza that it is given as an axiom (2a4). If the mind were not the idea of the body, the mind would not contain ideas of the ways that the body is affected by things. (Spinoza also makes a point of the fact that the body is a mode of extension and that the *ideatum* of the mind is not a mode of any other attribute other than the attribute of extension. This is one of the very few places in the *Ethics* where the odd doctrine of the infinitely many other unknown attributes shows up.)

Initial assessment of this account of the mind

This account of the mind solves a number of difficult problems in one ingenious stroke. Consider, for example, the problem of the union of the mind and body which had driven Descartes to the extravagances of the pineal-gland theory. Spinoza's account provides for a twofold relationship between mind and body without the necessity of introducing an inexplicable interaction between the physical and non-physical. On the one hand, the mind and the body are identical, since they are two ways in which one thing – a mode of substance – is expressed. On the other hand, there exists an epistemic relation between the two, since the mind, as idea of the body, is knowledge of the body.

In ordinary language, of course, it sounds strange to speak of the mind's *being* knowledge of something. We would normally speak in terms of the mind's (or simply our) *having* knowledge of something. This is one of those cases in which Spinoza would hold that ordinary language leads us astray, for it seems to presuppose that there is something – perhaps an underlying substratum or faculty – which is the mind and which 'has' ideas and hence knowledge. In Spinoza's view there is nothing 'underlying' my ideas except the divine thinking power of which the ideas that make up my mind are a finite expression. The human mind is not a faculty of understanding, nor a receptacle of ideas. On the contrary, it *is* ideas, where ideas are understood not as images, but as finite ways in which (so to speak) God thinks. I do not *have* a mind or *have* ideas, any more than I *have* a body. Rather, I *am* a complex physical entity (a human body) and a mind which is the complex idea of that body.

It is clear that Spinoza's account of the mind has promise for dealing with some tough questions. But along with the strengths of the theory, there are also some *prima facie* difficulties with the view. For example, according to the parallelism, each extended mode has a corresponding mode of thought – an idea of the extended mode. The idea of a human body turns out, on Spinoza's theory, to be a human mind. Since every mode of extension – every tree, every candle and every piece of paper – has a corresponding idea, does that mean that every tree, every candle and every piece of paper has a mind? Spinoza does not hesitate to admit that in a sense the answer is 'yes'. He says, 'the things we have shown so far are completely general and do not pertain more to man than to other

Individuals, all of which, though in different degrees, are nevertheless animate' (2p13s).

This is a remarkable claim, and it has been interpreted in very different ways by different readers. First, it should be noted that the word that is translated as 'animate' is the Latin word '*animata*'. In Latin, the term 'anima' means 'soul' or sometimes 'mind'. So Spinoza is saying that everything is 'besouled' or 'minded'. Nowadays we sometimes use terms derived from the root 'anima' (animated, animal) to mean 'alive'. In any case, whatever is meant by the term 'animata', a look at the other important phrase makes it pretty clear that Spinoza does not think that trees and rocks are perceiving themselves with thoughtful awareness. *In different degrees* all things are *animata*. But what distinguishes these differing degrees? Spinoza says that minds will differ from each other just as their *ideata* – the extended modes of which they are ideas – differ from each other. Some are more complex than others. Some are more excellent than others. He cannot explain in detail, he says, but in general he can say that '... in proportion as a body is more capable than others of doing many things at once, or being acted on in many ways at once, so its mind is more capable than others of perceiving many things at once'.

This is all quite abstract at this stage, but an important point has been made. If we would understand the mind better – i.e. the idea of the body – we must understand the body itself better. And with that Spinoza interrupts the discussion of the mind in order to explain more about bodies – what they are and how they act – about the attribute of extension and the laws that govern the modes of that attribute. The axioms, lemmas and postulates that are inserted between Propositions 13 and 14 constitute a brief and basic course in 'natural philosophy' – physics as Spinoza understood it in his day.

Study questions

1. How does Spinoza's theory of the mind help to solve the problems that plagued Descartes' view of the mind–body relation?
2. How does Spinoza avoid the conclusion that every rock and every tree has a mind?

The science of extended bodies – the physical interlude between 2p13 and 2p14

In his correspondence Spinoza indicates that he intended to write a full treatise on physics.[5] His death at the age of forty-four prevented him from realizing that intention, but the general outline of his views can be discerned in the principles included here in the *Ethics*. All physical things have some features in common just by virtue of the fact that they are modes of extension. The most important of these is the fact that they are in motion (to a greater or lesser degree) or at rest (A1, A2). In fact Spinoza holds that what distinguishes one body from another is a difference in their respective degrees of motion (L1).

At what we might call the 'micro-level' (Spinoza calls this the level of 'simplest bodies' [L7d]), small particles are in constant interaction – running into one another, bouncing off, stopping each another, communicating their motion to each other, etc. So the motion of a single simple body – which is definitive of what that body is – is the result of its interactions with other bodies. Relying on 1p28 Spinoza asserts that 'A body which moves or is at rest must be determined to motion or rest by another body, which has also been determined to motion or rest by another, and so on, to infinity.' And from this he derives (L3Cor) the following principle of inertia: '... a body in motion moves until it is determined by another body to rest; and ... a body at rest also remains at rest until it is determined to motion by another'. (Early in Part 3 of the *Ethics* we will see that this inertial principle takes on absolutely central importance in Spinoza's ethical system.)

All of this is recognizably Cartesian in origin – and it would have been familiar enough to readers acquainted with the 'mechanical philosophy' of the seventeenth century. Spinoza's originality lies not in these basic principles of natural philosophy, but in the way he embeds these in the larger metaphysical system and in the way he uses them in support of his ethical project.

After stating and elaborating a couple of basic principles that characterize the motion of simple bodies (A1″ and A2″), Spinoza turns his attention to those larger and more complex bodies which are made up of simple bodies – *corpora composita*. Composite bodies are defined as follows:

READING THE TEXT

> When a number of bodies, whether of the same or of different size, are so constrained by other bodies that they lie upon one another, or if they so move ... that they communicate their motions to each other in a certain fixed manner, we shall say that those bodies are united with one another, and that they all together compose one body or Individual, which is distinguished from the others by this union of bodies.

A composite body is an individual because of the constancy of interrelation – the 'fixed manner' of motion and rest among the many simple bodies that make it up. Sometimes Spinoza speaks of the 'ratio of motion and rest' among the parts (L5). There has been a lot of speculation over just what the phrase 'ratio of motion and rest' is supposed to mean here. We can say with some confidence that it refers to the relative position and motion that the parts of the complex body have *vis à vis* one another – position and motion that are definitive and constitutive of the composite body's form and which must remain more or less constant if that body is to remain the body that it is. Indeed – and this is the important point – the composite body's remaining the body that it is is *nothing other than* its parts maintaining this constancy of 'ratio of motion and rest' as they interact with each other and as the whole body interacts in various ways with the surrounding environment. Since it is this constancy of ratio of motion among the parts that is definitive of the individual, it follows that the individual can retain its identity and its individual nature even if specific simple bodies are replaced with others – so long as the ratio of motion and rest among the parts remains the same (L4). So, too, the individual as a whole can move (L7) or can become larger or smaller (L5) while retaining its identity – so long as the ratio of motion and rest among the parts, which is definitive of the individual, remains the same.

Before moving ahead, a few characteristics of Spinoza's account of composite bodies deserve emphasis, for they provide the basis for his understanding of the human body as an *organism*. In an article entitled 'Spinoza and the Theory of Organism', Hans Jonas pointed out that Spinoza developed his theory of composite bodies in such a way as to accommodate the biological processes characteristic of a living organism.[6] The significant defining factor is not the identity of the constituent parts. Were this the case, organic processes such as metabolism, nutrition and excretion would threaten a composite body's identity. Nor is spatial location in itself a significant factor, for locomotion of an organism requires that its identity be independent of where it is. Finally, the lack of emphasis upon size as a defining characteristic allows for a body to grow without losing its identity. Spinoza's account of what makes a body the body that it is was fundamentally influenced by his conception of the active living organism and its identity through the various changes that it undergoes in interaction with the environment. It is important to note, though, that while Spinoza is most interested in living organisms (since all of this is in service of his account of the human body and mind), this theory is applicable to all individual extended things. We find here impressive evidence of Spinoza's naturalism. The same structural and explanatory categories are to be applied to all finite things in nature – including human beings as a part of nature.

To say this, though, is not to say that there are no meaningful differences among extended things. On the contrary, the schema that Spinoza has provided allows for distinctions of a certain sort that are developed in the Scholium to Lemma 7. The 'simplest bodies', whose very identity is their specific motion (or lack thereof), can undergo no change in that motion without, in a sense, undergoing a change in their very identity. It can thus be said that at this level there is constant coming-to-be and destruction of things as interactions occur. At the level of composite bodies, though, there can be interaction with other things without destruction of the individual, for the individual is defined in terms of the 'ratio of motion and rest' among the parts, which can remain constant within the individual even if the specific motion of the specific parts is changed – for provision can be made in other parts of the system to maintain the ratio. A very complex composite of composite bodies can undergo any number of changes in its simplest and in its composite parts without thereby losing its individual nature. The human body is, of course, a very complex composite body which can remain itself while undergoing innumerable changes – including all those changes involved in metabolism, growth, motion, etc. Spinoza considers this ability to maintain identity through diverse changes an excellence on the part of the composite body.

Just as individual human bodies are understood to be complex composites made up of smaller composite bodies of diverse nature, so too the human individual can be seen as part of a yet larger whole. 'And if we proceed in this way to infinity, we shall easily conceive that the whole of nature is one Individual, whose parts, i.e., all bodies, vary in infinite ways, without any change in the whole individual' (L7sch). Since the whole of nature, so viewed, would be capable of undergoing endless changes without losing its definitive character, this infinite composite entity must be accounted most excellent.

This final point reminds us, once again, that Spinoza is providing an account of physical things (i.e. finite modes under the attribute of extension) that applies equally to tiny corpuscles, to human organisms, to ecosystems, to the planet as a whole and to astronomical nebulae. We human beings are a part of nature, and as such, we are describable in the same categories and subject to the same laws as all the rest of nature. Our bodies are indeed excellent in their remarkable capacity to survive – to maintain organic integrity – through all kinds of interactions with the environment. But this excellence is a matter of degree, and every composite body, in order to count as an individual thing at all, must manifest this capacity to some extent.

Spinoza concludes the 'physical interlude' with a set of six 'Postulates' summarizing some very basic facts about the human body and its interactions with the environment. For example, the human body is a composite mode made up of lots of composite modes of varying natures, hard and soft (Post. 1 & 2). The body is affected by many external things and the body can, in turn, move things around and in various ways have an effect on things external to itself (Post. 3 & 6). Finally, the body, in order to survive, needs nourishment and sustenance from the things around it – food, water and air to breathe (Post. 4).

Study questions

1. Spinoza holds that what distinguishes one composite body from another is the 'ratio of motion and rest' among its parts. Explain how this is an especially useful principle of individuation when dealing with living organisms.
2. Spinoza's physics is a version of the new 'mechanical' philosophy of nature that came to prominence in the seventeenth century. In what sense might it be called 'mechanical'?

Human knowledge (1) – Imaginatio

a. Sense-perception and memory (2p14–2p18)

Before delving into Spinoza's account of knowledge (and error), a little review would be in order. Early in Part 2 it was established that there is an infinite order of finite modes under the attribute of extension – an endless orderly series of material things that we call 'nature' and of which our bodies are a part. In addition, there is an infinite order of ideas under the attribute of thought – an endless orderly series of finite acts of thinking that we can collectively call 'the mind of God' and of which our minds are a part. We can say, a little misleadingly, that these two orders of modes under the two attributes run exactly parallel to each other, for Spinoza says that 'the order and connection of ideas is the same as the order and connection of things' (2p7). To speak of parallelism is misleading, though, for in fact there is only one order of modes, now conceived through the attribute of extension and now through the attribute of thought.

The human mind is the complex idea of the human body. This is Spinoza's account of what a mind is, and together with his account of complex composite bodies it affords an explanation of what makes my mind distinct from someone else's mind. This account of the mind also provides the basis of Spinoza's theory of human knowledge – and of human ignorance and error.

As a result of the parallelism/identity, the human mind contains ideas of whatever happens in the human body – i.e. the mind perceives what happens in the body (2p12). Since the body is constantly interacting with things around it, and thus being affected by those things, the mind is constantly perceiving the changes in the human body that result from those interactions. The human body, being highly complex and made up of many parts, is capable of being affected in lots of different ways, each of which will be perceived by the mind (2p14).

With these doctrines Spinoza has ingeniously laid the foundation for his account of sense perception. Things in the world produce changes in our bodies, and our minds (the complex ideas of our bodies) thereby contain ideas of those changes (i.e. perceive those changes). In more contemporary terminology we might describe it a little differently. We might say that stimuli from the environment impinge upon our sensory organs and produce changes in those organs and in the brain (i.e. excitation of the rods and cones in the retina followed by patterns of neuron-firings in the visual cortex of the brain) – changes which then register in our awareness. Spinoza knew nothing of rods, cones or neurons, of course, but the general idea – that we perceive things by registering in our minds the changes that are caused in our bodies by sensory stimuli – is right on target.

As soon as he provides this basic outline of how sense perception can occur, Spinoza begins to point out the fundamental limitations that make such perception so problematic and so unreliable as a source of knowledge. In 2p16 he contends that in the idea of the way my body has been affected by something else, the nature of my body and the nature of the object affecting me are both involved. So when I perceive some thing in the world around me, the idea in my mind is not directly an idea of the object I am perceiving. Rather, it is an idea of the way that my body is affected by that object. And that idea reflects the nature of the object in the world *together with* the nature of my own body (2p16c1). Spinoza even says, in the second corollary to 2p16, that our perceptual ideas reflect the constitution of our own bodies *rather than* the nature of the external bodies. This last claim actually goes too far, for it suggests that the idea of the way my body is affected by an external object is *more* a result of the nature of my body than the nature of the perceived object. This claim is more than Spinoza is entitled to. The point is just that the nature of the external object and the nature of my own body are both reflected – together – in the perceptual idea of the way my body is affected by an object. As we will see later, since I am unable to distinguish between the contribution made by my own body and that made by the external body, this kind of perception is often the source of confusion. Spinoza mentions in 2p16c2 that he has already given a number of examples of this in the Appendix to Part 1 (discussed on pp. 44–6 above).

To revert for a moment to more contemporary terminology we can say that our perceptual experience of the world is a joint product of (1) what is out there in the world and (2) the nature of our own perceptual apparatus. In visual experience, for example, our eyes are capable of registering only a certain part of the electromagnetic spectrum (that part that we call 'visible light') and of seeing only objects of a certain size. Our visual experience of the world is in great part a result of these characteristics of our sense-organs – and this experience can be quite misleading if we take it to reflect the way things truly are. Spinoza knew nothing of electromagnetic frequencies of course, but he did understand that the make-up of our senses and our nervous system profoundly affects our sensory experience of the world.

Spinoza explores this point a little further in the next few propositions. For example, if some object causes a certain change in my body, my mind will register that change and I will regard the object as present to me. My body will remain in this new condition until it is changed by some further influence. Thus, Spinoza argues, my mind will continue to have the idea of the way my body was affected and hence I will continue to regard the object as present to me until something else produces a different change in my body that indicates the absence of the first object (2p17). Spinoza also uses this sort of example to explain how we can continue to regard an experienced object as present after it is gone or has even ceased to exist (2p17c).

The demonstration of this last point is interesting, for it reveals that Spinoza was on a promising track, but also just how primitively mechanistic were the resources he had to work with. He wants to say something about the changes that occur in the percipient's body as a result of his or her perceiving something. But of course he knows nothing of the actual physiological and functional detail of the human nervous system. So he speaks of the 'fluid parts', driven by the externally perceived object to 'impinge upon the softer parts' and thereby 'alter the surfaces' of those softer parts and deflect the fluid parts in a different way (2p17cdem). The altered surface can then also serve as what we would call a memory trace, so that the next time the fluid parts are moving, they will be deflected in the newly altered way and the mind will again think the external object present. The physiology in this account is hopelessly antiquated, of course, but Spinoza's general point is quite correct. Sense-perception is the mind's awareness of the way the body is affected by objects in the world, and it is as much a reflection of the nature of our sensory apparatus as it is of the nature of the perceived object.

Spinoza calls this entire process of perceptually registering the presence of something via a modification of the body or brain 'imagination' (*imaginatio*). Note that in his terminology the term covers all sense-perception, and not just what we would call imagination (though it includes the latter as well). '... [W]e shall call the affections of the human body, the ideas of which represent external bodies as if they were present to us, the "images" of things, even though they do not reproduce the shapes of things. And, when the mind regards things in this way, we shall say that it "imagines"' (2p17Sch). Spinoza emphasizes that these images do not 'reproduce the shapes of things', for he does not want the reader to be thinking in terms of little pictures in the head. The images are indeed traces registering in the brain in the process of perception, but they are not pictures.

The Scholium to 2p17 is important for two additional points. Spinoza clarifies the difference between two senses in which we might use the phrase 'the idea of Peter'. On the one hand, there is the mode under the attribute of thinking that is the parallel correlate to the extended mode that is the body of Peter. (Actually it is the same mode of substance as Peter's body, but under the attribute thinking, rather than extension.) This idea – the idea of Peter's body – is Peter's mind (or, as Spinoza puts it more carefully, it 'constitutes the essence of the mind of Peter'). This is the 'idea of Peter' in the proper sense (we might say). But there is also the imaginational 'idea of Peter' that someone else (say, Paul) might have. This idea, while it does in a sense *involve* Peter's body, is really not an idea of Peter, but an idea of the way Paul's body is affected by Peter. In fact, Spinoza says, it reflects more the constitution of Paul's body than Peter's.

The fact that our imaginational ideas of things reflect the nature of our own bodies at least as much as the nature of the bodies that we are perceiving will be important for Spinoza's account of error. But at this point he begins to prepare us for that account by emphasizing that the mind does not err from the mere fact that it imagines. Even in those cases in which the mind imagines something as present that is no longer present (as in 2p17c), the imagining in itself does not 'contain error'. On the contrary, the imaginative idea is an accurate reflection of the way in which the body was affected by something. If, while having that idea, we also had an additional idea indicating that the putatively perceived object was no longer present, these ideas could co-exist in the mind with no contradiction. So the imaginational idea is not false *per se*. We will hear more about Spinoza's account of error below.

2p18 provides Spinoza's account of memory and, by extension, of that part of human psychology that can be explained by the principle of association. If we have experienced two things simultaneously in the past, then whenever one of them is imagined (either experienced via the senses or just conjured up in what we – today – would call the imagination), we will immediately recollect the other. So if, when I met Susan, she was standing under a pear tree, then when I see or think of Susan, I will remember the pear tree. The demonstration relies on the same mechanical account of the imagination offered in 2p17c.

Spinoza takes this occasion of the Scholium to remind the reader that the imaginational/perceptual idea I have of Susan does not reflect the true nature of Susan, but only the way in which my body is affected by her. He also makes a further important point. The association between my thought of Susan and my thought of the pear tree is based entirely on the fact that I happen to have experienced the two simultaneously in the past. There is no intrinsic logical connection between Susan and a pear tree, nor is there any similarity between them. So, too, in the case of words. Spinoza points out that a Roman, upon seeing an apple, will immediately think of the word *pomum*, though there is no intrinsic connection or likeness between the word and the fruit. It is just that the Roman has often heard the word while seeing the fruit, so they have become associated in his mind. So each of us will pass from one thought to another, depending on what sorts of experiences we have had in the past. Seeing a horse's footprint in the sand, a soldier will think of a horseman and war, whereas a farmer will think of a plough and a field. Each of us will have an order of associations in the imagination resulting from our past experiences. We will soon learn from Spinoza that there is also another kind of association among ideas that follows a different order – not the fortuitous order in which each of us happens to have encountered things in experience, but the order of the intellect, which is alike in all of us.

Study questions

1. Why does Spinoza say that our imaginational (perceptual) ideas of things indicate the nature of our own bodies as much as they indicate the nature of the objects of our perception?
2. What is the difference between the idea of Peter's body that constitutes Peter's mind and the idea of Peter's body in Paul's mind?

3. According to Spinoza how does a word (such as 'apple') come to be associated with a specific type of thing (i.e. a certain kind of red fruit)?

b. Ideas of ideas (2p20–2p22)

Setting aside 2p19 for a moment (we will come back to it), let us turn to the next three propositions, 2p20–2p22. Rather unexpectedly Spinoza introduces here the claim that there are not only ideas of extended modes, but also ideas of those ideas. We are told that the idea of an idea (*idea ideae*) is related to the first-level idea just as that first-level idea is related to the extended mode of which it is an idea. The main difference consists in the fact that the first-level idea and its *ideatum* are modes of different attributes, whereas the idea and the *idea ideae* are both modes of thought: 'the idea of the mind and the mind itself are one and the same thing which is conceived under one and the same attribute, viz. thought ... the idea of the idea is nothing but the form of the idea insofar as this is considered as a mode of thinking without relation to the object'.

This is an odd doctrine, and it raises all kinds of questions. These questions and the voluminous controversy in the secondary literature need not concern us here, but two features of this doctrine deserve mention. First, the existence of the *idea ideae* makes it possible for Spinoza to speak of our having awareness of certain intrinsic characteristics of ideas themselves. This proves important for the programme of intellectual improvement, for it makes it possible for us to recognize the intrinsic adequacy or inadequacy of certain ideas. Secondly, the doctrine of the *idea ideae* allows Spinoza to accommodate the experience of reflexive self-awareness within his system. After all, I am not only aware of the way my body is affected by other things, but I am aware of my very awareness thereof. There are a number of problems here, but one positive aspect of Spinoza's doctrine of the *idea ideae* is that it allows for self-awareness without positing a substantial self. Ideas are, so to speak, transparent to themselves, but this does not require that there be a self to which the ideas are transparent.

c. Inadequate cognition and the limitations of *imaginatio* (2p11c, 2p19 and 2p23–2p31)

1. Introduction: the centrality and difficulty of the problem of error

The theory of *imaginatio* outlined in 2p14–2p18 is not only the first stage in Spinoza's explanation of human knowledge; it also provides the basis for his account of falsehood, and of human ignorance and error. Though we have not emphasized this point up to now, the question of how we human beings can make mistakes and hold erroneous beliefs is a major problem for Spinoza's philosophy. We know from 2p7c (and Spinoza will explicitly remind us in 2p32) that God's idea of some thing (i.e. the idea of the thing in the infinite modal order under the attribute of thought) is the very thing itself, expressed ideationally rather than in extended form. The idea in the divine intellect agrees entirely with its *ideatum*. It is a true idea and it is embedded in the nexus of ideas which are its causes – ideas that reflect the nexus of causes in the order of extended modes. But *all* ideas – including the complex idea that is the human mind – are ideas in the divine intellect. If the human mind is part of the infinite intellect, and if all the ideas in the infinite intellect are true, how can it be that we human beings err in our thinking? To put it more bluntly – if my ideas are God's ideas, and if God's ideas are all true ideas, why are my ideas not always true ideas?

This problem is especially acute for Spinoza. A few decades earlier, Descartes had faced a similar version of the problem of how we human beings err. He offered a plausible-sounding solution in terms of human free will. According to Descartes' view we fall into error because we use our free will to assent to things for which we have insufficient evidence. On this view, the understanding merely apprehends things, and such apprehension cannot be false (or true either, for that matter), for it is not, in itself, a judgement – i.e. it affirms nothing. But we, by the power of our unconditioned free will, affirm or deny things and thus risk (and often fall into) error. This is a plausible-sounding way to explain how error arises, but it is not open to Spinoza, for two reasons. First (and most importantly) Spinoza denies that there is any free will at all. Secondly, on Spinoza's view ideas themselves are characterized by affirmation or denial – they are, so to speak, already judgements.

Before considering Spinoza's solution to this puzzle we should pay attention, for a moment, to the peculiar character of the problem itself. Most philosophers find it challenging to explain how we human beings can achieve knowledge and truth. For Spinoza, the bigger challenge is to explain how we could ever fall into error. Spinoza has this unusual problem because his God is absolutely ultimate and all-encompassing, and yet there is no obvious place for imperfection in his God.[7] Nor is the problem of human error the only place in Spinoza's philosophy where this sort of problem arises. On the contrary, a significant part of the *Ethics* is occupied with the attempt to answer the following sorts of questions:

> How can there be passivity when in fact there exists only God and God is perfectly active?
> How can there be time when in fact there exists only God and God is eternal?
> How can there be bondage when there exists only God and God is perfectly free?

Spinoza attempts to solve these problems (as have other philosophers of a more Platonic sort) by denying that there are in fact ultimately any of the imperfections mentioned in these questions (e.g. passivity, time, bondage). The apparent existence of these imperfections is then explained by reference to our nescience and error. But given Spinoza's view of the mind this nescience and error is itself hard to explain. Thus the centrality and importance of the problem of error. And hence the centrality and importance of the doctrine of the imagination.

2. The inadequacy of our cognition (2p11c and 2p19)

All of God's ideas are true. All of our ideas are God's ideas. Yet some of our ideas are not true. How can this be? Part of the solution to this conundrum is already in place in our discussion of the *imaginatio* as the ideas of the ways in which the body is affected by things. For the other essential piece of the puzzle we need to return to an important earlier passage that was mentioned and then set aside prior to our discussion of the physical interlude (on p. 54). The passage in question is from the corollary to 2p11 and it occurs right after Spinoza has made the point that the human mind is a part of the infinite intellect of God. The one long sentence deserves detailed examination:

Therefore, when we say that the human mind perceives this or that, we are saying nothing but that God, not insofar as he is infinite, but insofar as he is explained through the nature of the human mind, or insofar as he constitutes the essence of the human mind, has this or that idea; and when we say that God has this or that idea, not only insofar as he constitutes the nature of the human mind, but insofar as he also has the idea of another thing together with the human mind, then we say that the human mind perceives the thing only partially, or inadequately. (2p11c)

This difficult sentence is best understood as follows: since the human mind contains the ideas of various things, God has the ideas of certain things simply by having the complex idea that is the human mind. But merely 'having' the idea of something in this way is not enough to provide adequate cognition of the thing. God does of course have adequate cognition of the thing, but he does not have that adequate cognition merely in virtue of his having the idea that is the human mind. God has adequate cognition of the thing by having the idea that is the human mind *and also* the idea of another thing. Since the human mind often does not include the idea of the 'other thing' which is required for God's (adequate) idea of the initial thing, the human mind perceives the thing only inadequately. But what is this 'other thing'?

Recalling Axiom 4 of Part 1 ('The knowledge of an effect depends on and involves the knowledge of its cause'), we can best interpret the 'other thing' referred to in 2p11c as the cause (or better, causes) of a given thing. On this interpretation the inadequacy that characterizes a certain human perception would be the result of the fact that the human mind does not include the ideas of the causes of the thing perceived. The idea which God has of the thing, however, is an adequate cognition of the thing, for it includes not only the idea included in the human mind, but also the ideas of the causes of the thing whose idea is in the human mind.

It is helpful to remember that for Spinoza causation is akin to logical implication, and that effects follow from causes as conclusions follow from premises. Axiom 4 of Part 1 tells us that we do not really (i.e. adequately) know a thing or a fact if we do not know the causes that have conditioned it to be as it is. Spinoza says that to have an idea of a thing without knowing its causes is like having a conclusion without the premises from which the conclusion follows.

READING THE TEXT

In Spinoza's view this is a truncated sort of understanding that misses the connections among things and fails to see the timeless structural order that underlies all things. Such cognition fails to know things as they are and is hence not wholly true. Spinoza calls such cognition 'inadequate'.

In 2p19 Spinoza brings this analysis directly to bear on the mind's cognition of the body. The human body, as we know, is conditioned to be and to act by numerous causal determinants (both vertical and horizontal). Spinoza speaks of these as the 'great many bodies by which [the human body] is, as it were, continually regenerated'. God's adequate idea of the body includes not only the human mind (in one sense the 'idea of the body') but also the ideas of the causes of the human body. Relative to God's idea of the human body, then, the human mind can be seen as an inadequate idea of the body, for it does not include the ideas of the causes of the body. This is precisely the argument that Spinoza makes in the demonstration of 2p19 (relying explicitly on 2p11c).

This is the best way, I think, to read the passages under consideration. But this interpretation is not without its difficulties. Given that all things in the horizontal modal order are at least tenuously causally connected (1p28 and 2L3), some commentators (Joachim, for example) have held the view that only the infinite idea of the whole of reality – the *infinita idea Dei* – can be considered adequate, since only it encompasses all the elements of the causal order. This view holds an element of truth, though it should not lead us to despair with regard to the possibility of human knowledge. On the contrary, we must only realize that adequacy is a matter of degree – a point that Spinoza reinforces by his repeated use of the Latin term *quatenus* in this context – a word meaning 'in so far as' or 'to the extent that'.

So Spinoza's explanation of how we can be in error is based on the fact that our understanding is incomplete and partial. The human mind is indeed part of the mind of God, but the emphasis is on the word *part*. Our minds in themselves are ideas taken out of context, foreground images without background, or (Spinoza's preferred analogy) conclusions without premises. The inadequacy of ideas in our minds consists in their isolation and partiality. These same ideas, embedded in the nexus of ideas that reflect the causal order of nature – i.e. these same ideas as they are in the mind of God – are entirely adequate and true.

Study questions

1. Why is it difficult, for Descartes and for Spinoza, to explain error? How did Descartes solve the problem?
2. Why, in Spinoza's theory, is the human mind's knowledge of the body 'inadequate'?
3. How could I make my mind's knowledge of my body more adequate?

3. The limitations of imaginatio (2p23–2p31)
The next nine propositions emphasize (1) the extent to which our cognition of things consists of *imaginatio* – i.e. of the ideas of the ways in which our bodies are affected by other things – and (2) the extent to which that cognition is inadequate.

For starters we only know our own bodies by means of the ideas of the ways in which they are affected by other things. As we saw above (in the discussion of the demonstration of 2p19), our minds do not constitute adequate knowledge of our bodies, for we do not have in our minds the ideas of the causes of the existence and survival of our bodies. Spinoza tells us that we do not even know of the existence of our bodies except through the ideas of the ways in which our bodies are affected by other things (in Spinoza's terminology, 'the ideas of the affections of the body') (2p19). Moreover, the same arguments that establish the inadequacy of our knowledge of the body explain why our minds do not involve adequate knowledge of the parts that make up our bodies (2p24). And since the mind only knows itself by means of the ideas of the ideas of the affections of the body (2p23), the mind's knowledge of itself is as inadequate as the mind's knowledge of the body (2p29).

In the earlier discussion of *imaginatio* we noted that the idea of the way my body is affected by some object in the world involves both the nature of my body and the nature of the external object. But (to put it in the technical terminology of the last section) the adequate idea of the object is not in God insofar as God constitutes my mind, or constitutes the idea of the way my body is affected by the object. On the contrary, the adequate idea of the object is in God insofar as God has the idea of the object and also the ideas of all the other things that have caused that object to be. So my imaginational idea of the way my body is affected by some object does not involve adequate knowledge of that object (2p25).

2p26 establishes that we only know that an object actually exists if that object affects our bodies (i.e. if we perceive it via *imaginatio*). But since we can imaginatively perceive things even after they are no longer present or even no longer exist (2p17c), we cannot gain an adequate knowledge of the duration of things (2p31). And since the continued existence of our own bodies depends on numerous causes and factors of which we have no adequate knowledge, we will have only an inadequate knowledge of the duration of our own bodies (2p30). Our imaginational knowledge of actually existing things and of the causal connections among these things is so inadequate that they will appear to us as if they were uncaused and indeterminate. We will call them corruptible and contingent, though all this can really mean is that we are unable to say how long they will endure or whether they will exist at a given time. Spinoza takes this opportunity to remind the reader that it was proven in Part 1 that absolutely everything is completely causally determined and that there is no real contingency in nature at all (2p31c).

The ideas of the *imaginatio* follow one another in a haphazard fashion, depending on what objects the individual's body happens to be affected by as he or she moves through the world. These ideas involve both the nature of the external bodies and the nature of the perceiver's body, confusedly and indistinguishably co-present. Spinoza calls this 'perceiving things from the common order of nature'. In an important sentence he summarizes the conclusions that he has drawn in his investigation of the confusion and limitations of the *imagination*: 'From this it follows that so long as the human mind perceives things from the common order of nature, it does not have an adequate, but only a confused and mutilated knowledge of itself, its own body and of external bodies' (2p29c).

This needs to be emphasized. The ideas of the *imaginatio* provide our initial cognitive access to the world around us, and to our own bodies and minds. Deriving mostly from sense perception and associative memory, this kind of cognition also includes hearsay as well as what we would call 'imagination' today. It is a valuable mode of access to the world, for it is only by physically interacting with things and having ideas of the ways they affect our bodies that we come to know of the actual existence of things at all (2p26). As Spinoza will explain in Part 3, our emotional lives are also conditioned and deeply influenced by the ideas and associations of *imaginatio*. And yet, as important and as pervasive as this type of cognition is, it is profoundly unreliable and provides the mind with 'only a confused and mutilated knowledge of itself, its own body and of external bodies'. Elsewhere Spinoza refers to this kind of cognition as being in a 'waking dream'.

The reader is left in a discouraging position at this point. The only sort of knowledge that we have learned about (*imaginatio*) has been shown to be wholly inadequate. If this is all that we human beings are capable of, then we are condemned to ignorance, confusion and passivity as we form inadequate ideas based on our chance encounters with things. But of course this is not the only kind of cognition available to us. Spinoza offers just a hint of the alternative – a ray of light in the darkness – in the Scholium to 2p29:

> I say expressly that the mind has, not an adequate, but only a confused knowledge of itself, of its own body, and of external bodies, so long as it perceives things from the common order of nature, i.e. so long as it is determined externally, from fortuitous encounters with things ... and not so long as it is determined internally, from the fact that it regards a number of things at once, to understand their agreements, differences and oppositions. For so long as it is disposed internally, in this or another way, then it regards things clearly and distinctly, as I shall show below.

Just what this other source of knowledge is, in which the mind is 'determined internally', the reader is not told at this point. In 2p37 we will begin to learn of the way human beings can acquire adequate knowledge. But first Spinoza needs to wrap up a couple of loose ends on the subject of falsehood and error.

Study questions

1. Why does sense perception (imagination) provide us with only 'a confused and mutilated knowledge of itself, its own body and of external bodies'?

4. Falsehood and error (2p32–2p36)
With the extensive discussion of the inadequacy of the ideas of the *imaginatio*, Spinoza has the pieces required to solve the puzzle of falsehood and error. We are reminded that of course insofar as they

are related to God, all ideas are true (2p32). To speak of ideas 'insofar as they are related to God' is to speak of them as they are fully embedded in the mind of God – i.e. as they are in their causal nexus in the infinite modal order under the attribute of thought. In this context every idea is true, and there is nothing about them that could warrant their being called false (2p33). And to the extent that an idea is in an individual human being's mind in the same way that it is in God's mind, that idea will likewise be true in the individual's mind. (Spinoza explicitly references 2p11c again when making this point.) So the only possible source of falsehood is the fact that ideas are often in our minds in a way that is different from the way ideas are in God's mind. And that difference is a function of the fact that a human mind is only a tiny part of the divine mind – a part that does not encompass the many causes that give the idea as it is in God's mind its completeness, its causal nexus, its context, and hence its adequacy and its truth. Spinoza sums up the doctrine in 2p35: 'Falsity consists in the privation of knowledge which inadequate, or mutilated and confused, ideas involve.'

Knowing that there may be questions in the reader's mind, Spinoza provides two examples of the way in which the lack of knowledge of the causes of things can generate falsehood and error. Neither of these examples is entirely satisfactory, but they do help us to grasp how the author understands the doctrine he is defending. (1) The first example is a favourite of Spinoza's: human beings think that they are free – i.e. that they can either act or not act on a given occasion – because they are aware of their actions but unaware of the causes of those actions. Since I know that I made a decision but do not know of the causes that determined me to decide as I did, I think that there were no such causes and chalk it up to my 'free will'. But Spinoza says that this 'free will' is nothing more than an empty phrase that papers over the lacuna in my causal understanding. The falsehood is nothing positive, he argues, but merely a privation – a lack of knowledge. (2) The second example occurs more than once in Spinoza's writings, and has been widely discussed in the secondary literature. When we look at the sun we imagine it to be about 200 feet away from us. According to Spinoza the imagining itself is not an error. In fact the imaginative idea is not actually false – rather, it accurately reflects the way in which a person's body is affected by the sun. If we knew enough about the causes of that affection – i.e. about the sun, about our visual perceptual powers, about optics, etc. – we would still have the same imaginational idea, but would no longer erroneously believe that the sun is 200 feet away. On the contrary, we would have a true idea of the way the body is affected by the sun, embedded in a nexus of true ideas about astronomy, optics, physiology of perception, etc. No error had to be dispelled, for the error was nothing positive. Again, Spinoza holds that the error consists only in the absence of the full causal understanding.

These are ingenious examples, and especially in the case of the perception of the sun it seems plausible to think of the error as a matter of insufficient knowledge of the larger causal context. But as many critics have rightly pointed out, the belief that the sun is 200 feet away is not just the absence of the belief that it is 93 million miles away. Error is the positive belief in something that it is in fact false. And while Spinoza is correct in saying that the imaginational affection of the body will remain the same even after we have extensive knowledge of astronomy, etc., the false belief that the sun is 200 feet away – i.e. the error – will not remain the same. Indeed, it will have to be dispelled. And that should be enough to tell us that Spinoza's account of error as 'nothing positive' has difficulties. So, too, with the first example. To be unaware that my actions have causes is one thing; to think that they are caused by my free will is another. While the former might indeed be describable as 'nothing positive', the latter could not.

Spinoza's attempt to account for error purely in terms of 'the privation of knowledge which inadequate, or mutilated and confused, ideas involve' is not entirely satisfactory. But it led him to interesting insights about the centrality of the body in perception and the importance of the idiosyncracies of our sensory apparatus. And it represents an impressive attempt to find a way to include our mistakes and errors in a thought-world that consists entirely of God's ideas, all of which are entirely true.

Study questions

1. Spinoza holds that even after I learn about optics and astronomy and my own perceptual apparatus – and even after I learn that the Sun is 93 million miles away – my imaginational (visual) experience of the Sun will not be changed. Is he right about that?

2. Spinoza's theory allows him to hold that error is ignorance – i.e. that error is nothing positive, but is rather just a lack of knowledge. What problems are there with that view?

Human knowledge (2) – Reason (Ratio) and intuitive knowledge

a. The common notions

After the long treatment of *imaginatio*, the account of the more reliable and adequate modes of cognition is surprisingly brief. In fact, the third and highest kind of knowledge is barely mentioned, almost in passing. But these kinds of cognition are crucial, for they provide the way out of the confusion that besets the *imaginatio*.

Spinoza tells us that there are certain things (though 'things' is an odd word here) that are 'common to all things and ... equally in the whole and in the part of all things'. These things, since they are common to all, do not constitute the essence of any singular particular thing (2p37) and, most importantly, can only be conceived adequately (2p38). Since they are grasped adequately, any additional ideas that follow logically from them will also be understood adequately (2p40).

In these few propositions Spinoza provides the basics of his account of 'the second kind of knowledge'. The doctrine hinges on the notion of that which is 'common to all things and ... equally in the whole and in the part of all things'. But what is he talking about, and above all, why does he think that we will have an adequate understanding of these things?

To answer this question we need to remember, again, that the confusion characteristic of the *imaginatio* is partially a result of the fact that the idea of the nature of the external body and the idea of the nature of my own body are confusedly co-present in the idea of the way my body is affected by the external body. Not having an adequate idea of my own body or the external body, I am unable to distinguish the contribution made by the external body and that made by my own, so long as I have only the idea of the modification of my body (i.e. as long as I know things only via *imaginatio*). But Spinoza claims that such confusion cannot arise with regard to that which is common to all things and equally in the whole and in the part of things. For example, extension is common to all extended things, and manifests itself equally both in the whole and in the parts of all extended things. So, though the idea of the nature of an external thing will only be confusedly present in the idea of a modification of my body by that thing, the idea of extension itself will suffer no confusion. In having the idea of the modification of my body I will necessarily have an unconfused idea of extension. Certain ideas, then, are adequate in everyone's mind – for example, the ideas of extension and of motion – for all extended things are characterized by extension and motion, and there is no way for confusion to infect the ideas of the way our bodies are affected by things.

Spinoza calls the ideas of these common things the 'common notions', and it is with these ideas that reason (or the 'second kind of knowledge') begins. There has been considerable controversy about just what ideas Spinoza includes among the common notions. It is clear that he includes extension and motion, for he cites Lemma 2 as he speaks of the fact that '... all bodies agree in certain things' (2p38c). Presumably under 'extension' he would have understood the principles of geometry and under 'motion' the basic laws of motion and rest that he laid down in the section on physics (after 2p13). In the terms developed in Part 1 we could say that the common notions include ideas of the attribute of extension, and the immediate and mediate infinite and eternal modes that follow from the attribute.

Two surprising consequences of this view need to be considered before we move ahead. Earlier, in discussing the infinite and eternal modes, we suggested that they might best be understood in terms of the laws of nature – i.e. that they be thought of as the law-like ways in which physical nature always and everywhere acts. On this reading, though, Spinoza would be suggesting here in Part 2 that each of us, just in virtue of the fact that his body is affected by other things in the environment, has an adequate understanding of the basic laws of nature. That astonishing claim would make no sense at all if offered today as a description of the scientific sophistication of the man on the street. But it seems less wildly implausible if we remember that Spinoza was a seventeenth-century rationalist, influenced by Descartes, who believed that extended reality is ultimately mathematically/geometrically structured. The axioms of Euclid describe fundamental ways in which God/nature acts extendedly, just as do the principles of motion dealt with after 2p13. From Plato's doctrine of recollection to Descartes' innate ideas, mathematics has long been held to be an *a priori* science, and the presence of mathematical/geometrical ideas in the minds of all people is good traditional philosophical doctrine. Spinoza's version – that adequate ideas of the basic geometrical laws of nature are involved in the idea of every modification of the human body – is unusual, but the underlying doctrine is not.

We noted that the common notions include ideas of the attribute of extension. The astute reader will remember that the attribute reveals the very essence of God (it is 'that which the intellect perceives of substance, as constituting its essence' 1D4). In light of this, it seems that Spinoza believes that every person has an adequate idea of the essence of God. This seems like an extravagant claim, but it is indeed exactly what Spinoza wants to say – and does say very explicitly in 2p45–47. 2p47 concludes, 'The human mind has an adequate knowledge of God's eternal and infinite essence.' In evaluating this remarkable claim we should remind ourselves that Spinoza's God is not the remote and inscrutable quasi-personal *mysterium* of traditional theology. The eternal and infinite essence of God is the power of nature, expressed always and everywhere in mathematically describable, rationally knowable law-like ways. To oversimplify a little, we could say that if we can understand geometry and thus grasp extension (of which geometry is the science), we *eo ipso* have an adequate idea of the infinite and eternal essence of God.

The common notions can be called universals, for they are ideas of that which, being common to all things, is universally present. But Spinoza is very much concerned that the reader not confuse these common notions with universals as traditionally understood. The latter, he says, are the result of the fact that the human perceptual system is limited in the number of distinct images it can form of things. So, for example, if I encounter lots of human beings and my body is affected by all of them (in perception), I will form many different images of many different people. But my capacity to form such images will eventually be exceeded, the images will become indistinct, and I will begin to imagine only those features that they all agree in (since these are the features that are impressed upon me by every perceived individual). Thus I form the confused universal concept 'man' and associate certain common features with that universal. Spinoza emphasizes that cognition based on these universals is highly confused and unreliable. Moreover, it varies widely from individual to individual for each of us forms universals in light of his or her individual experience:

For example, those who have more often regarded men's stature with wonder will understand by the word *man* an animal of erect stature. But those who have been accustomed to consider something else, will form another common image of men – e.g. that man is an animal capable of laughter, or a featherless biped, or a rational animal (2p40s1).

These traditional definitions are confused, and it is no wonder that they have led to disagreements: '... it is not surprising that so many controversies have arisen among the philosophers, who have wished to explain natural things by mere images of things' (2p40s1).

Study questions

1. Why are the 'common notions' not subject to the confusion that besets *imaginatio* (sense perception)?
2. One might respond that it is crazy to think that every person has an adequate knowledge of the basic laws of nature. How might Spinoza (as a seventeenth-century scientist) respond?
3. If someone today were to say that every person has an adequate idea of the essence of God, it would sound very strange. What is it about Spinoza's view that makes this claim seem less odd?
4. How do the common notions (of which we necessarily have adequate knowledge) differ from the less reliable universals (which are confused and misleading)?

b. The three kinds of knowledge

In a second Scholium to 2p40 Spinoza provides a brief summary of the two types of cognition that he has considered thus far, and tantalizingly mentions a third. The three-part classification system that he offers here is quite similar to versions offered in other of his writings (*Short Treatise* and *TdIE*), though there are some differences as well. In the *Ethics*, which we will be focusing on, the lowest grade of cognition is called 'knowledge of the first kind, opinion or *imaginatio*'. It includes sense-perception, as discussed above, as well as knowledge that we get from language and signs. This sort of imaginational knowledge is '... mutilated, confused and without order for the intellect', and is quite unreliable (for all the reasons recounted at length above).

READING THE TEXT

The second kind of knowledge (reason), on the other hand, is based on the common notions, as explained in the last section, and on 'the adequate ideas of the properties of things' (2p40s2). Spinoza does not specify just which properties he has in mind, but presumably (since we can have adequate ideas of them) they are the properties that can be described and understood mathematically and geometrically (rather than those, discussed in the Appendix to Part 1, that result more from the nature of the perceiver than from the nature of the objects perceived).

In addition to these two kinds of cognition we are told that there is another, third kind, which is called 'intuitive knowledge'. The description of this one is maddeningly cryptic and abstract: '... this kind of knowing proceeds from an adequate idea of the formal essence of certain attributes of God to the adequate knowledge of the essence of things'.

Spinoza attempts to illustrate and explain all three kinds of cognition with a single example – finding the fourth proportional when given three. For example, 16 is to what number as 4 is to 3? In fractional notation: $4/3 = 16/?$ A merchant will readily figure this out by multiplying 16 times 3 and then dividing that product (48) by 4 to get 12. The merchant can do this although he may not have any real understanding of proportionality, for he heard the rule in his younger years and remembers to apply it now. This represents knowledge of the first kind. Alternatively one might understand basic mathematical principles regarding proportionality (derivable from Euclidean fundamentals). This would be an instance of deductive inference based on wholly understood universal mathematical truths – a case of reason or knowledge of the second kind. Or finally, in very simple cases, one has an immediate intuitive grasp of the proportional relationship between two numbers (say, 1 and 2). Having that grasp, and confronted with the number 3, one can instantly see that 6 would be the number which, when paired with 3, would represent the same proportion as 1 to 2. This is offered as an example of intuitive knowledge, or knowledge of the third kind.

The example of the proportionals is helpful in illustrating the differing ways in which one might arrive at an answer to a mathematical problem. But it does not provide the kind of general clarification that the reader might want – especially regarding the third kind of knowledge. Spinoza has little more to say about the third kind of knowledge at this point, but it will become important near the end of the *Ethics*. We will have occasion to return to the question of just what makes this kind of cognition so special when we encounter it again in its important role near the end of Part 5.

The most important thing about the third kind of knowledge at this point is a characteristic that it shares with the second kind of knowledge. What we cognize by means of either one of these – reason or intuition – is true and we truly know it. To know something in either of these ways is to know it as it follows from the most fundamental ways in which God/nature acts. It is to know a thing as an expression of the divine active power (*natura naturans*) and as a part of the natural order (*natura naturata*). To know something this way – embedded, as it is, in the causal nexus – is to know it as it is in God. And to know something in this way is to know it as God knows it, for to say that an idea is adequate in my mind is just to say that the idea is in God in so far as God constitutes my mind (2p11c). This kind of knowledge reveals to us what real knowledge is, and its adequacy provides the standard for what counts as knowledge (2p42). In a famous passage in the Scholium to 2p43 Spinoza says, 'As the light makes both itself and the darkness plain, so truth is the standard both of itself and of the false.'

It is noteworthy here that Spinoza seems entirely untroubled by the doubt and scepticism (methodological and otherwise) that plague Descartes throughout the early parts of his *Meditations*. Spinoza would attribute most of Descartes' difficulties to the fact that he starts with himself and the contents of his own mind rather than starting with that which is inherently most knowable – i.e. with God. We have seen that Spinoza thinks that our initial ideas of our bodies, our minds and the external world are woefully confused and inadequate. It is no wonder that Descartes, who started with the contents of his own mind, had such difficulties resolving his epistemological problems and became stuck in a possibly vicious Cartesian circle. Spinoza would say that to pretend, as Descartes does, that one finds even simple mathematical truths uncertain is to pretend that one cannot tell light from darkness and to undermine one's project from the beginning.

The second kind of knowledge (reason) knows things as they truly are. Spinoza concludes his discussion of this way of knowing by reminding us of a couple of characteristics of things as they truly are. We learned in Part 1 that all things follow with absolute

READING THE TEXT

necessity from the power of God. Reason, therefore, which knows things as they are, will regard things as necessary, and not as contingent (2p44). In this context Spinoza explains that our tendency to regard things as contingent results from the vagaries and vacillations of the *imagination* (2p44c1 and 2p44c1s).

Finally, in 2p44c2 we are told that, 'It is of the nature of reason to perceive things under a certain species of eternity.' This phrase – under a certain species of eternity (*sub quadam specie aeternitatis*) – is perhaps the best-known phrase in all of Spinoza's philosophy. People who know very little of Spinoza might yet have heard that he would have us see things *sub specie aeternitatis* (sometimes translated as 'under the aspect of eternity' or 'under a form of eternity'). In the demonstration of 2p44c2 the eternal aspect derives from the necessity: '... this necessity is the very necessity of God's eternal nature'. All things can be understood as following from the eternal divine nature with the timeless necessity characteristic of logic and mathematics. Thus, to the extent that we know them as they are in God, we know them in a way that makes no reference to time. Reason provides that non-temporal perspective in which things can appear in the light of eternity.

Reason can reveal things as they are in God only because it is founded on the common notions which reflect the ways that God timelessly and everywhere acts. As we noted above, the common notions include the idea of the attribute of extension. Indeed, the idea of anything whatever necessarily involves the idea of the attribute of which it is a mode. The attribute in turn is that which the intellect perceives as constituting the divine essence. Thus the fact that we humans are capable of having knowledge of the second kind, or reason, demonstrates that the human mind has a knowledge of God's eternal and infinite essence (2p45–47). We discussed this remarkable claim above (p. 79), but Spinoza places it here as the capstone of his discussion of reason and its power to know things truly as they are in God.

Study questions

1. According to Spinoza, to know things by means of reason (and also intuition) is to know them as necessary and to know them under a form of eternity. What is the connection between necessity and eternity?

Rejection of free will (2p48 and 2p49)

Part 2's lengthy discussion of the human mind has provided an extensive account of the mind's powers of cognition. At the end of the discussion, in two propositions followed by a lengthy Scholium, Spinoza takes up the question of the mind's power of volition – i.e. what is commonly referred to as the will. He proceeds in two stages. First, in 2p48, he argues that what we call the mind's acts of willing consist of modes of thinking, and that as modes they are of course determined by other modes (horizontal and vertical) in the causal order. Then, in 2p49 and its Scholium he targets Descartes' account of what is involved in our affirming or denying the truth of some idea – i.e. accepting something as true or rejecting it as false. Spinoza's view on this question is (and was) one of the most controversial aspects of his philosophy, and he takes the time to discuss a number of possible objections that could be raised against his view.

2p48 begins, 'In the mind there is no absolute, or free, will ...' What, exactly, is this 'absolute, or free, will' whose existence Spinoza is denying? It is an entirely familiar notion, but not so easy to sum up in a sentence. Perhaps it is best explained by an example. On the bicycle route from my office to my home there is an intersection where I must either go left or go straight. Either way will bring me to my home in about the same amount of time, though one route is a little shadier, whereas the other is a little safer due to there being less traffic. Each day I must choose one route or the other, and I do not always choose the same one. Whenever I choose to go straight, I do so in the belief that I could also have turned left. It seems to me, at the moment at which I choose to go straight, that it was entirely possible for me to have chosen to go left. I have the sense that by a mere act of will I can decide to go one way or decide to go the other – and while I know that certain considerations or influences might incline me, on a given day, to go straight, even on those days I think that I could, by an act of will on my part, decide to go the other way. Implicit in my belief that I could choose to go in either direction is a belief that there are not, at the moment of choice, causes present in me or in the environment that are sufficient to necessitate my going straight. I think that my will – my power to choose – while perhaps influenced by various factors, is not ultimately determined by prior causes. It is in this sense I think that I possess a free will.

READING THE TEXT

Spinoza knows that many people believe that they have this kind of freedom of the will, but he thinks that they are mistaken in that belief. In fact, as we noted above (p. 75), this is one of his favourite examples of how we make mistakes because we do not have sufficient knowledge of the causes of things (2p35s). We think that we have free will because we are aware of our actions but ignorant of the causes by which we are determined to act. For Spinoza every mental act, such as a decision or affirmation, is a mode of thinking – i.e. a mode of substance under the attribute of thought. And as we learned in Part 1 (1p28 and 1p29), every finite mode is determined to be as it is by another mode, and that one by another, *ad infinitum*. No mode can render itself undetermined (1p27).

Now that we have learned more about Spinoza's account of the relationship of the mind and the body, we can see the point even more clearly. We now know some of the details of the body's makeup and its interactions with other things in accordance with the laws of motion. We have no reason to doubt that that is an entirely deterministic process. But since the mind is the idea of the body (2p13s) and the order and connection of ideas is the same as the order and connection of things (2p7), we can see that the causally determined character of the body in its interactions with other things is mirrored in the mind as well.

In a famous letter (Letter 58 to Schuller) Spinoza uses an example of a stone thrown through the air to illustrate his views on our beliefs about our freedom. The stone receives an impulsion to move from some cause (say, a person throwing it). It will continue to move through the air as a result of its inertial tendency (which Spinoza calls its endeavour to continue moving). All of this, of course, is entirely in accordance with the laws of nature. Now imagine that the stone can think and that it is aware of its endeavour (its inertial tendency) to continue moving. It would think that it is completely free, '... and that it continues in motion for no other reason than that it so wishes'. Spinoza concludes that, 'This then is that human freedom that all men boast of possessing.'

In the Scholium to 2p48 Spinoza explicitly denies that there is any faculty of will at all. Of course there are individual volitions, but that should not lead us to think that there is a volitional faculty. Likewise he notes that there are ideas, but there is no faculty of intellect which produces them. Spinoza argues that the belief that there are faculties in the mind is a result of our misleading tendency to form abstract universals. So he says that '... intellect and will are to this or that idea, or to this or that volition as "stoneness" is to this or that stone, or "man" to Peter or Paul'.

So far Spinoza has argued that there is no free will and that there is no volitional faculty. That should be sufficient to settle the matter, but in the final proposition of part 2 he focuses critically and at length on a specific view held by his influential predecessor, Descartes. Descartes believed that we have an absolutely free faculty of will by means of which we make our decisions about how to act and what to do. But he also famously held that this free will plays a central role in connection with what we *believe*.[8] On this view, we entertain ideas with our intellects, but there is no affirmation of the idea's truth or rejection of it as false until we choose (by means of an act of will) to affirm or deny it. So, for example, my senses might communicate to me a visual impression of the Sun as a glowing ball two hundred feet away. I am entertaining the idea of a glowing ball two hundred feet away, but there is not any belief or affirmation that there is a glowing ball two hundred feet away unless and until I decide (by an act of free will) to affirm this idea as true.

In 2p49 Spinoza explicitly rejects his predecessor's view for two reasons. First, he denies that there exists any faculty of free will of the sort that is required for this Cartesian story. Secondly, he claims that every idea involves its own affirmation, and hence that there is no need for a separate volitional act to affirm an idea as true. To take the example of my visual idea of the Sun, Spinoza claims that this idea is inherently affirmative, and that in the absence of any other ideas I will indeed believe that there is a glowing ball two hundred feet away. It is of course possible for me not to come to believe that there is a glowing ball two hundred feet away, but not as a result of my choosing, via free will, not to affirm the visual idea as true. On the contrary, if I do not come to believe it true it will be because I have other ideas (of optics, of astronomy, of the psychology and physiology of perception) in light of which I am not taken in by the illusory visual idea. In fact, in light of these additional ideas I can come to affirm the truth of the visual idea as an idea of the way in which my body, with its idiosyncratic perceptual system, is affected by a middle-sized star ninety-three million miles away.

In a lengthy Scholium to 2p49 Spinoza considers a number of

possible objections to his position and answers them from the perspective that he has developed at length in Part 2. He knows that his position is complex and difficult, and that its implications may not be immediately clear to the first time reader. But he is confident that his view is the right one, for it sees the human being in the context of the larger natural order – as a part of nature rather than as a pretender to the status of 'kingdom within a kingdom'. After this lengthy examination of the human mind and its powers of cognition, Spinoza is prepared to turn his attention to our emotional lives – the subject of Part 3 of the *Ethics*.

Study questions

1. Spinoza holds that our volitions are determined by prior causes as are all other things and events in nature. And he holds that since our volitions are determined in this way, there is no such thing as free will. Is he right in this latter claim?
2. Descartes held that in order for us to believe something to be true (for example, that there is a desk in front of me), we must decide, by means of an act of will, to affirm it as true. Spinoza denies that we do any such thing. Who is right about this?

PART 3 – ON THE ORIGIN AND NATURE OF THE AFFECTS

By the end of Part 2 the basic metaphysical concepts and categories of Spinoza's system are in place. The reader has learned how all things follow necessarily from the infinite and eternal substance. The first principles of physics have been established and an account offered for the origin of the human mind. We have learned how human beings are capable of gaining knowledge, but also why we are so often subject to ignorance and error. Free will has been shown to be illusory – a misleading notion that we form as a result of our lack of understanding.

In Part 3 Spinoza begins to make good on the title of his work, for he begins to address the fundamental questions of ethics. Spinoza's approach to ethics is not exactly the same as that of many theorists of our own day, for he is not chiefly concerned to establish what actions are right or wrong, just or unjust. He is not uninterested in those questions, of course, but for him they are secondary – they are questions whose answers will be apparent once we have addressed the more fundamental ethical issue.

Spinoza's conception of ethics is closer to that of the ancients. He wants his ethical investigation to establish what the best kind of life for a human being is, and how we can overcome the obstacles that keep us from living such a life. In pursuing these questions he will also have occasion to talk about other issues that are of interest to ethicists today. For example, he will take a stand on what are called 'meta-ethical' questions – questions about the very meaning of ethical discourse – about what we mean when we say of something that it is 'good' or 'bad'. He will briefly discuss the role of the state and of religion in producing and sustaining normative attitudes and beliefs. He will offer descriptive observations about the motives and practices of ordinary people. But for Spinoza all of this is secondary to the main task at hand – discovering (and demonstrating) what kind of life is best for a human being, and how we can attain to such a life.

One should not think, as we go forward, that in turning his attention to the question of ethics Spinoza is turning away from the metaphysical and epistemological questions that occupied us at such length in Parts 1 and 2. On the contrary, the abstract metaphysical account of God and of the relationship between God and individuals in nature is directly relevant to the ethical project. In fact, it will turn out that rightly understanding God (and ourselves as parts of God) is an essential requirement for achieving the good life. And as we will see, Spinoza derives his ethics directly from his theory of human nature – a theory whose foundations are rooted in the intricacies of Part 2.

In order to address the ethical question, Spinoza turns his attention to the affects – or, as we would say these days, the emotions. His reasons for doing so are straightforward. He wants to know what sort of life is best for a human being. He holds, plausibly, that a life of joy is better than a life of sadness. But joy and sadness are emotional states, so the ethical investigation will have to take into consideration our affective lives. It will turn out that the good life is in part defined by positive emotions. In addition, certain other misguided and excessive emotions – irrational passions – can be serious obstacles to our achieving and enjoying the good life. If we would devise a strategy to free ourselves from the destructive negative passions and free ourselves *for* the positive affect of joy, we need to understand just what the affects are, how they arise and how they operate. Part 3 of the *Ethics* – 'On the Origin and Nature of the Affects' – is devoted to just that task.

Any number of earlier theorists had discussed the affects and the proper place of certain emotions in the good life. Plato, Aristotle and the Stoics (for example) all had important things to say on this subject. But Spinoza's treatment of the emotions is different, and he opens Part 3 with a brief discussion of what makes his approach unique. He notes that since our emotions often seem irrational, some authors seem to have thought that they are not susceptible to being understood at all. These authors often laugh at human emotional folly or bemoan the excesses to which people are led by their passions. They '... censure eloquently and cunningly the weaknesses' to which we are prone. But Spinoza is not interested in this kind of contemptuous denunciation. On the contrary, he sums up his view on this matter in a well-known passage from his *Political Treatise:*

> I have laboured carefully, not to mock, lament, or execrate human actions, but to understand them; and to this end I have looked upon passions, such as love, hatred, anger, envy, ambition, pity, and the other perturbations of the mind, not in the light of vices of human nature, but as properties, just as pertinent to it, as are heat, cold, storm, thunder, and the like to the nature of the atmosphere, which phenomena, though inconvenient, are yet necessary, and have fixed causes, by means of which we endeavour to understand their nature.

Human beings are a part of nature, and human emotions are natural events. Like all other natural events, they occur in accordance with the laws of nature and can be understood in terms of those laws. Spinoza will thus not deviate from his previously adopted method of exposition and demonstration. He will use the same geometrical method that he has used in Parts 1 and 2. '... I shall consider human actions and appetites just as if it were a question of lines, planes and bodies.'

Adequate and inadequate causes and ideas: acting and being acted upon (3d1 & 2; 3p1 & 3)

As he begins his account of the emotions, Spinoza needs to draw some basic distinctions that will be useful in the later development of the theory. In the first definition of this part (3d1) he presents the notion of an 'adequate cause' and distinguishes it from a 'partial or inadequate cause'. An adequate cause, we are told, is one '... whose effect can be clearly and distinctly perceived through it'. The point that Spinoza is making can be understood more easily if we remember that he tends to think of causation and logical implication as closely related. In a valid deductive inference, the premises are sufficient to guarantee the truth of the conclusion. The premises are enough (so to speak) to cause the conclusion to be true. In contemplating the premises one can see that the conclusion must follow from them. So too in the case of a causal relation. If a cause is sufficient, by itself, to guarantee that the effect follows, Spinoza says that the cause is an adequate cause of the effect.

This notion of adequate causation serves to ground Spinoza's understanding of activity and passivity, for in the second definition of Part 3 we learn that we can be said to act whenever something takes place (within us or outside of us) which follows from our nature – i.e. something of which we are the adequate cause. This doctrine is quite abstract at this point, but it is helpful to remember the account of *imaginatio* in Part 2. The ideas of the *imaginatio* are ideas of the ways in which someone's body is affected by other things in the environment. The individual in question is certainly not the adequate cause of these affections, for they are partially caused by things outside of the individual. Thus, according to 3d2, the individual can be said to be to a great extent passive (rather than active) in these instances. In contrast to these ideas of the imagination are the common notions – adequate ideas of those things that are present in everything and which are equally in the whole and in the part of things. These ideas are ideas of things that are complete within me, and thus I may be said to be the adequate cause of whatever follows from these ideas. So whenever anything follows from ideas that are adequate in my mind, I have been active (rather than passive) – I have acted (rather than having been acted upon). This is the point that Spinoza makes in the first proposition of this part (3p1) and repeats two propositions later (3p3). The human mind is more active the more it has adequate ideas and is less active the more its ideas are dependent on ideas of things outside itself.

Having established that our minds are active as a result of our adequate ideas and passive in light of our inadequate ideas, Spinoza leaves this promising line of thought for a while and goes in a different direction. He will pick up this thread later, in the middle of Part 4, where it will become very important.

Study questions

1. Being active and being passive are defined in terms of adequate and inadequate causation – which is defined, in turn, by reference to whether the effect can be clearly and distinctly perceived through the cause. Why does Spinoza think that there is a connection between something's being active and its effects being clearly and distinctly perceivable through it?
2. Why does Spinoza think that there is a connection between the adequacy of our ideas and the degree of our activity?

Reminder – No causal interaction between mind and body (3p2 & sch)

Spinoza knows that when most people think of the mind and how it can be active, they think of our decision-making and the way in which we decide to do things and then do them. Most people share with Descartes the view that a mental event (say, my conscious decision to make a phone call) can cause physical things to happen (say, my picking up and dialing the telephone). This is such a commonly held view that Spinoza interrupts his exposition in order to remind the reader that he has shown this view to be false. He has argued, early in Part 2, that modes under the attribute of extension must be explained and understood by reference to other modes of extension and not by modes under another attribute (such as thought). Mental things do not cause physical things to happen, and physical things do not cause mental things to happen. Rather, the two series of causes and effects can be thought of as running exactly parallel to each other. But that characterization, too, is misleading, for in fact there is only one series of modes which can be understood under the attribute of thought (as a series of ideas) or under the attribute of extension (as a series of physical things and events). So the decision to make a phone call is the mental expression of a physical process that has occurred in my body (presumably in the brain) and that will lead to my picking up the phone and moving my fingers to dial.

In the long Scholium to this proposition, Spinoza makes a very important point that is as relevant and timely today as it was in his own day. We tend to think that very complex human activities (such as building a building or writing a symphony) could not possibly be explained solely in terms of physical causes and processes, without any explicit mention of mental decisions, desires or deliberations. But Spinoza reminds us that no one yet knows the structure, function and workings of the body well enough to know what it is capable of and what it is not. He mentions also that lower animals, to whom we do not attribute higher cognitive processes, are nonetheless able to perform remarkable feats of physical coordination and prowess. And sleepwalkers, whose somnolent minds are presumably inactive, are nonetheless able to do complex tasks. All of these examples show that the body can do remarkable things on its own, '... simply from the laws of its own nature'.

Neuroscientists in our own day are only gradually coming to understand how the nervous system works and how the complexities of bodily motion, speech articulation and problem-solving can be the result of patterns of neuron-activations in the brain. The working assumption among these scientists is that it will be possible to understand what we do by reference to these physical causes. Spinoza was writing at the dawn of the scientific revolution, and of course knew nothing about nerves, neurotransmitters or the evolution of the brain. Yet he was confident enough about the trajectory of natural-scientific understanding to propose that we seek to understand our bodily motions and even our most complex behaviours in terms of physical laws and causes.[9]

Study questions

1. Spinoza thinks that it will be possible to explain every motion of a human being's body (including every intentional action performed by a person) by reference to physical causes alone. Do you think that he is right about this?

READING THE TEXT

Conatus (3p4–3p10)

In a sense, the first three propositions of Part 3 are just a kind of warm-up exercise – making points and drawing distinctions that will be of value later. The real argument of Part 3 begins with the series of propositions from 3p4 to 3p10. The centrepiece of this series is 3p6 in which Spinoza introduces the principle of *conatus* and claims that it is a universal characteristic of all things. The conatus principle will be absolutely central to the rest of the *Ethics* – to the affective psychology, the ethical theory and even the discussion of political theory. This pivotal principle deserves to be considered with care.

3p6 – What it says and what it means

The central proposition (3p6) reads: 'Each thing, as far as it can by its own power, strives (*conatur*) to persevere in its being.' On one level, this sounds like a straightforward claim about the instinct for self-preservation that is obvious in most of the animal kingdom. It is easy to see that most animals (humans included) generally act so as to prolong their existence and to avoid death and destruction. A number of earlier philosophers took note of this fact and some (the Stoics, for example) claimed that it represented a universal characteristic of human and animal life.

Spinoza of course wants his principle to cover this kind of survival instinct in animals, but 3p6 makes a much more universal claim. The assertion is that *each thing* (*unaquaeque res*) strives to persevere in its being. He seems to think that this principle can apply to rocks and clouds as well as cats and people. In order to understand what Spinoza means here we must look carefully at the words and think about how he arrives at this claim.

The term 'conatur', here translated as 'strives', normally has the connotation of someone's 'trying' or 'making an effort' to do something. This, in turn, suggests that the individual has a conception of what he or she is trying to accomplish. If we were to interpret 3p6 in this way, we would have to attribute to Spinoza the view that everything has a conception of its own perseverance in being, and is making an effort to bring it about. As we noted when discussing 2p13s, Spinoza does claim that everything is *animata*, but he does not think that everything is capable of the kind of conceptual sophistication required for having a conception of its own future and seeking to ensure the continuation of its existence.

Fortunately there is an alternative reading of the term 'conatur' that provides Spinoza with much of what his theory requires without implausibly attributing complex thoughts to rocks. In an earlier work Spinoza uses the terms 'conatus' or 'conatur' to refer simply to a body's natural tendency to move in a certain way. So, for example, he says that 'Every body that moves in a circle strives to move away from the center of the circle that it describes.'[10] This principle of (what we would call) centrifugal force presumably does not require that the body have a conception of the direction that it strives to go, nor that it 'make an effort' of any kind. Rather, to say that it strives to move in a certain direction simply means that it naturally tends to do so – i.e. that it will do so unless it is constrained in some way.

The science of motion in the seventeenth century provides another helpful example. Galileo and Descartes had both formulated versions of the principle of inertia – i.e. the principle according to which a body in motion will remain in motion unless affected from without (or if at rest will remain at rest unless affected from without). Here again there is a tendency for motion (or rest) to maintain itself unchanged, though there is presumably no intention or conscious effort involved. Spinoza holds that just as motion, by its own nature, tends to maintain itself, so too each existing thing in the universe tends to continue in existence unless adversely affected from without. In the case of highly complex and consciously reflective beings such as ourselves this tendency to persevere in being might well involve deliberation, intentional planning and conscious effort. But in the case of lower animals and non-living creatures, the conatus is just a natural tendency to continue in existence unless destroyed by something else.

3p6 – Why Spinoza believes it and how he demonstrates it

Spinoza bases his proof of 3p6 on the prior two propositions (3p4 and 3p5) and on very general abstract principles taken from Part 1. There has been extensive discussion in the secondary literature about how strong this demonstration is. But we can get a better understanding of what led him to this important principle by pursuing a somewhat different route. We can get clearer on his position by following up on the parallel, mentioned above, between the principle of inertia and the conatus principle.[11]

As we noted in the discussion of the physical principles after 2p13 (pp. 58–61 above), Spinoza first establishes a principle of inertia with regard to a simple body in motion (in the Corollary to L3). He then defines 'composite bodies' as those in which the parts maintain among themselves a certain constant 'ratio of motion and rest'. The composite body can grow or shrink, move from one place to another and replace some parts with others while still remaining the same composite body – so long as the ratio of motion and rest among the parts remains the same.

Note that the composite body exists because – and to the extent that – it maintains a constancy of ratio of motion and rest among its parts. We can say that it naturally tends to maintain that ratio because the constancy of that ratio is what defines it as the individual that it is. To put the point a little differently, it is impossible for this composite body not to maintain the ratio, for if it were to fail to maintain this ratio it would not be this composite body. So – to the extent that the parts maintain the ratio of motion and rest among themselves, the composite body exists. Its very existence consists in the maintenance of this ratio, so we can confidently say that it naturally and necessarily tends to maintain the ratio and hence that it naturally and necessarily tends to persevere in being. And this is just what 3p6 is claiming.

This way of thinking about it helps to explain some other parts of Spinoza's conatus doctrine. For example, 3p4 says that nothing can be destroyed except through an external cause. Spinoza can be confident that nothing in the composite body itself will destroy it, for the body is defined in terms of the maintenance of a certain relationship among the parts (the above-mentioned 'ratio of motion and rest'). Any ostensibly internal part of the composite body that is destructive of the defining ratio is *eo ipso* not in the requisite relationship to the other parts and is thus not a part of the body. Anything that might destroy the body will have to be something other than a part of the body – i.e. something external to the body.

Let us look at this from a more contemporary scientific viewpoint for a moment. Nowadays we know quite a bit about the biochemical processes that constitute and sustain the organic unity and continuity of an individual plant or animal. These processes all happen in accordance with the general laws of nature, of course, and they constitute the organism's survival and its continuity over time. Sometimes we say that an animal has a natural tendency to ingest nutrients, absorb oxygen, expel wastes, repair tissue damage, regulate body temperature, etc. But there is something a little misleading in saying that the animal 'has' a tendency to do these things. A more accurate way to describe it would be to say that these processes, occurring as they do, in coordination with each other, constitute the homeostatic maintenance of the organic unity that *is* this animal. These processes *are* the animal. The natural tendency of these processes to occur as they do amounts to a natural tendency on the part of the animal to survive – to persevere in being. This natural tendency will perpetuate the organic unity that is the animal just as the natural inertial tendency of a moving object keeps that object in motion. Once Spinoza has defined the identity of a composite body in terms of the constancy of the ratio of motion and rest among the parts of the body – and once it is clear that the parts naturally interact with each other in such a way as to maintain that ratio – it is easy for Spinoza to embrace the parallel between a moving body's inertial tendency to remain in motion and a composite body's tendency to persevere in being. Organic creatures such as plants and animals provide the most striking examples of the conatus principle, but Spinoza thinks that it will hold for any body.

This seems to me the best way to understand 3p6, and I think it likely that Spinoza was led to hold the principle, in its full universality, by something like this line of reasoning. But as mentioned above, the actual demonstration that he offers (i.e. the demonstration of 3p6) proceeds at a higher level of abstraction – at the level of general metaphysical principles that make no explicit mention of motion, of inertia, of organisms or of extended things *per se* at all. We will not enter into the many detailed controversies associated with the demonstration, but only look at the bare outline.

In 3p4 Spinoza claims that no thing can be destroyed except by an external cause. At first he says this proposition 'is evident through itself', but then, as if he fears his readers might not agree, offers a kind of argument in favour of it. 3p4 underwrites 3p5 which claims that things of a contrary nature (i.e. things that can destroy each other) cannot be in one and the same subject. This does seem to follow from the prior proposition. But Spinoza then claims that 3p6 – the crucial conatus principle – follows from 3p5 (plus a couple of very general metaphysical principles from Part 1). This step is less convincing. The idea seems to be that since nothing contains within itself anything by which it can be destroyed, 'each thing is opposed to everything that can take its existence away'. And from the fact that each thing 'is opposed to' whatever can destroy it, Spinoza concludes that each thing strives to persevere in its being.

There are numerous objections that one might raise to this line of reasoning, but the demonstration of the principle is less important than what it means and what Spinoza does with it. Spinoza sees a thing's striving to persevere in being as an active force or power – indeed, it is the individual's power to maintain its existence as it interacts with other things in the environment. Just as Spinoza equated God's power with His essence (1p34), so too he tells us that 'the power, or striving (*conatus*) by which [a thing] strives to persevere in its being is nothing but the ... actual essence of the thing itself' (3p7d). This striving has no internally imposed temporal limitations either. It is a striving to persevere in being for an indefinite time (2p8).

Study questions

1. How convincing is the implicit parallel that Spinoza draws between the physical principle of inertia and the biologically based self-preservation instinct?
2. Is Spinoza correct in suggesting that the physical existence of biological organisms (including ourselves) is just the homeostatic persistence and coordination of certain complex physical processes?

3p4 and 3p6 – Objections and replies

It might have occurred to the astute reader that there are some obvious objections to be raised against Spinoza's conatus doctrine. Before turning our attention to the role this doctrine plays in the theory of emotions, we should consider at least one of these objections – an important one. Spinoza holds that everything always strives (or tends) to persevere in being, and that nothing can be destroyed except by an external cause. But what about obvious counterexamples? Suicides, for example, are patent instances of self-destruction. Time-bombs and even the Sun itself (destined to burn itself out) have been offered as clear counterexamples to Spinoza's thesis.

Spinoza did not know anything about time bombs, of course, and he did not have anything to say about the Sun in this context. But he is aware that suicides constitute a problem for his view – so much so that he addresses the question on three different occasions in the *Ethics*. In the first passage (2p49s) he puts suicides in the same category as 'children, fools and madmen', and grants that he does not know what to think of such strange creatures. In 4p18s, discussing what reason demands of us, he asserts that 'those who kill themselves are weak-minded and completely conquered by external causes contrary to their nature'. This has to be Spinoza's way of responding, for only by removing the cause of the destruction from within the individual can he avoid the unwelcome conclusion that the individual was destroyed by itself (or by something within itself). But it is not clear just how we are to draw the line between that which is within the individual and that which is external to it. Spinoza provides a little more clarity on this question with the following examples in 4p20s:

> Someone may kill himself because he is compelled by another, who twists his right hand (which happens to hold a sword) ... or because he is forced by the command of a Tyrant (as Seneca was) to open his veins ... or finally because hidden external causes so dispose his imagination, and so affect his body, that it takes on another nature, contrary to the former ...

The last of these three examples cited by Spinoza is an interesting and tricky one, but a full discussion of it would take us too far afield. The main point is that in every case Spinoza offers a redescription of the situation that allows him to deny that the individual (or anything in the individual) was the cause of its own destruction. However convincing (or unconvincing) the reader might find these redescriptions, this is what Spinoza must say if he is to hold consistently to the *conatus* principle.

The three basic affects – desire, joy and sadness (3p9s and 3p11s)

As we noted above, the striving by which each individual endeavours to persevere in its being is the individual's actual essence. It is the force or power by which the individual maintains its existence as it interacts with other things. When things occur that can be explained as following from that force or power, we say that the individual acts (applying 3d2). From my bodily striving to persevere in being it follows that my temperature remains roughly normal, that I breathe, that I eat, that I pursue those things that are conducive to my self-preservation. My mind likewise strives to persevere in its being by striving to affirm ideas of the continued existence of the body (for the mind is the idea of the body). Spinoza explains in 3p9s that '... when this striving is related only to the mind, it is called will; but when it is related to the mind and the body together, it is called appetite. This appetite therefore, is nothing but the very essence of man, from whose nature there necessarily follow those things that promote his preservation. And so man is determined to do those things.' In the next sentence we learn that when we are conscious of the appetite, it is called desire.

So what we call 'desire' is a manifestation of our basic conatic striving to persevere in being as a psycho-physical organism. This essential striving is at the root of all our desires and all our actions.

3p11 reminds the reader that when the body's power of acting is positively or negatively affected by something, the mind's power of thinking will be likewise affected. This is not a surprise, of course, for the parallelism/identity guarantees that occurrences in a complex extended mode will be reflected in the complex idea of that mode. But this proposition is important, for it introduces the crucial notion that an individual's power of acting – physical and mental – can be increased or diminished. Spinoza also speaks of the individual's 'passing to a greater or a lesser perfection'. What, exactly, does he have in mind here?

Focusing for a moment on the physical side, it is clear that Spinoza does not mean that the characteristic 'ratio of motion and rest' that is definitive for the individual's body is changed. What can change, though, is the body's ability to maintain itself with that characteristic ratio as it interacts in potentially disruptive ways with other things in the environment. The 'power of acting' can be thought of, on the bodily side, as a kind of organic vitality that might include a high energy level, an intact immune system and a robustly healthy constitution. That kind of power makes it possible for one to interact vigorously with the environment – to affect and be affected by external things – without losing one's bodily integrity. And Spinoza would remind us that the body's ability to interact in various ways with other things is reflected in the mind's capacity for more responsive and more adequate thinking.

The body's and mind's powers of acting can be diminished – by disease, by injury, by infirmity, or similar factors. Likewise these powers can be increased by exercise, by nutrition, by education or by any number of positive influences. When, as a result of encountering a destructive factor of some kind, the mind's power to act is diminished, this transition to a lower state of perfection is sadness (*tristitia*). When the mind passes to a higher degree of power, the transition is called joy (*laetitia*) (3p11s).[12] Since we want to persevere in being, we naturally want to raise our power of acting and naturally want to avoid any diminution of that power. So, as Spinoza points out, we naturally pursue that which causes joy and naturally avoid that which causes sadness.

When my body is being affected by some thing in the environment, I perceive that thing – i.e. my mind has an idea of the way that thing is affecting my body. In the terminology of Part 2 my mind *imagines* the thing. Since I naturally strive to increase my body's power of acting, I naturally strive to have my body affected by things that will enhance that power (i.e. things that cause joy). On the mental side we can say that I strive to imagine those things that increase my body's power of acting (i.e. that cause joy) (2p12). And when I encounter and imagine things that diminish my power of acting (i.e. that cause sadness), my body naturally strives to escape or destroy them, and my mind naturally strives to imagine things that do away with them (3p13). All of this naturally follows from our conatic striving to persevere in being.

Explaining and cataloguing the emotions (3p13–3p59 and Appendix)

Desire, joy and sadness are the three basic affects in Spinoza's theory. They can be conjoined with certain ideas and with each other to produce a nearly endless catalogue of further emotions. For example, if I experience joy and I have an idea that a certain person or thing is the cause of that joy, I will love that person or thing. According to Spinoza love just *is* 'joy, with the accompanying idea of an external cause' (3p13s). Since I naturally strive to increase my power of acting, and the object of my love causes such an increase (i.e. causes joy), I will desire to have the beloved thing or person present as much as possible. If that desire is thwarted by some other thing or person, I suffer sadness with the accompanying idea of an external cause, an emotional state that Spinoza defines as hatred (3p13s). If that cause injured the object of my love, my hatred is called indignation (3p22s). If that cause removed the object of my love by causing the object of my love to love that cause more than me, my hatred will be called jealousy (3p35s). The possibilities of developing further emotions out of the basic three are endless, and Spinoza exploits these possibilities in insightful and ingenious ways throughout Part 3 of the *Ethics*.

This example accurately shows Spinoza's view of the ways the affects can build on one another, interact and be modified by changing circumstances. But the example is somewhat misleading, for it suggests that the objects of our emotions (of love, hate, etc.) really are the causes of the joy and sadness involved therein. In fact, though, since we are dealing here with modifications of the body and with the mind's ideas of these modifications, these ideas are subject to inadequacy and error. Through association, superficial similarity, and other sources of confusion, we often have affective reactions of love or hate to things that do not, themselves, directly cause joy and sadness. For example, when one thing (X) causes me sadness, but it is associated in my mind with another thing (Y) because I have, by chance, often experienced them together in the past, the experience of Y by itself will provoke sadness in me and I will hate Y even though it is not a direct cause of sadness in me (3p15dem). Or if the mind perceives some (possibly superficial) likeness between A and B, and if A really does cause us sadness, we will also feel hatred toward B. In these ways, 'Anything can be the accidental cause of joy, sadness or desire' (3p15). Through the intricate interplay of the affects it often happens that we have, at one time, contrary emotions toward the same thing – we may love it and hate it, experiencing vacillation (3p17s). Little wonder that Spinoza views human beings as '... driven about in many ways by external causes ... like waves on the sea, driven by contrary winds, we toss about, not knowing our outcome and fate' (3p59s). Part of the ethical task, of course, will be to establish some order and direction in this emotionally tempestuous confusion.

Reading through the extensive catalogue of emotions that Spinoza provides in Part 3 is fascinating, and not really difficult. The connections and interrelations that he discerns among seemingly disparate emotional states can be eye-opening. He hints at the affective basis of social relations in general as he points out, in case after case, how our emotional responses are affected by our perception of the responses of others. He offers an interesting explanation of the mixed feelings that accompany the sense of *schadenfreude* (3p26 & 3p47). The remarkably graphic account of the sadness-inducing fantasies of the jilted lover suggest that Spinoza may have had first-hand experience with that green-eyed monster we call romantic jealousy (3p35s). And he makes the interesting (and important) claim that our love or our hatred for something or someone will be more intense if we imagine that thing or person to be free, than if we conceive it to be necessary.

At the end of Part 3 Spinoza provides, in a kind of Appendix, a serial list of the affects, offering a formal definition of each. The content of this section is not significantly different from the etiological accounts of the different emotions developed in the various propositions and scholia of Part 3, but they are ordered in a different way and some additional explanation is offered. For example, we learn something of the importance of parental instruction in moral education (Def. 37 Exp.) and about why humility is such a rare trait in human beings (Def. 29 Exp.).

Study questions

1. Is it plausible to hold, as Spinoza does, that there are certain basic emotions (i.e. desire, joy and sadness) which can be treated as the 'building blocks' in developing a science of all emotions?
2. What does Spinoza mean by 'accidental' when he says that 'Anything can be the accidental cause of joy, sadness or desire' (3p15)?
3. Has Spinoza succeeded in his avowed aim to develop a science of human emotion that investigates our affective life 'just as if it were a question of lines, planes and bodies'?

Preliminary Account of Good and Evil (3p39s)
Before leaving Part 3 two remaining points should be addressed, for they are intrinsically important, and because they will ease the transition to Part 4. Back in 3p39 Spinoza began discussing the circumstances under which one would be inclined to do evil to another, as well as the likely emotional response if one believes that another is doing evil to oneself. Since this is virtually the first use of the phrases 'doing evil' and 'doing good', Spinoza pauses to define these terms. 'By good I understand every kind of joy, and whatever

leads to it ... And by evil every kind of sadness.' What is good is thus a function of our emotional response to things. If something is conducive to the growth in our power to act – our physical and mental flourishing – then it is good. 'So each one, from his own affect, judges or evaluates what is good or bad ...' In the Preface to Part 4 we will hear more about these normative terms, and Spinoza will develop a somewhat less purely subjective view. But he will not waver in his view that the standards for good and evil are not to be sought in the Scriptures or indeed anywhere else but in our human thriving.

Active and passive emotions (3p58 & 59)

The last two propositions of Part 3 introduce an important distinction between active and passive emotions. Most of the emotions that have been discussed are cases in which some external factor causes an increase (joy) or a decrease (sadness) in a person's power to act. These are rightly called passions, for we are passive recipients of these causal influences. The emotions are caused in us – we do not cause them ourselves. But there are also other cases in which we ourselves can cause an increase in our own power to act. When we contemplate our own strength, for example, it brings joy. These can be called active emotions, for they are a result of ourselves and our own natures. Since our nature or essence is an active endeavour to maintain or increase our power, it follows that no emotion that marks a transition to a state of lesser power (i.e. no sadness) can be a consequence of our nature alone. So no active emotion can be a sad or painful emotion. Thus, since we want to maximize joy and minimize sadness, we would do well to maximize the extent to which our emotions are active, rather than passive. In Spinoza's system, of course, this kind of internal self-determination is not only a reliable path to joy. It is also, by definition, freedom.

Study question

1. According to Spinoza, only passive emotions can be sad or painful. Why is this?

PART 4 – OF HUMAN BONDAGE, OR THE POWER OF THE EMOTIONS

The *Ethics* promises to explain what kind of life is best for a human being and how an individual can overcome the obstacles that prevent her from having that kind of life. Thus far Spinoza has provided an elaborate causal account of the nature and origins of the emotions, but very little in the way of normative judgments – positive or negative – regarding those emotions or the actions and attitudes that they involve. Near the end of Part 3 he offered a preliminary definition of 'good' that ties it closely to joy (3p39s). The brief discussion of active emotions (as opposed to the passions) clearly has some normative import as well (3p58). The description of passion-ridden humanity as 'tossed about by the waves of the sea, and driven by contrary winds' certainly conveys a negative judgement. But as yet Spinoza has not provided a systematic account of normative ethics – an account of how we should live and what sort of life is best – and why. Part 4 of the *Ethics* will address these questions directly.

The title says that Part 4 will be about human bondage and the power of the emotions. In fact, though, that title is misleading. While a fraction of this Part deals directly with the power of the emotions (up until 4p18 or thereabouts), the larger part consists of an explanation of the proper meaning of the terms 'good' and 'evil', an assessment of which emotions are good (and which ones evil) and an account of the actions and affects of an ideal type of individual whom Spinoza calls 'the free man'. Along the way Spinoza explains the foundations of virtue, the value of social life and cooperation, and the origins of the state. This is not just a grab-bag of disparate topics, for there are logical connections among them. But the content of this Part extends well beyond what is announced in the title. It is noteworthy that twice – once at 4p18s and once in the lengthy Appendix – Spinoza provides an overview of the outline of the argument to make the connections more transparent to the reader.

Spinoza is right in thinking that a summary can be helpful in following the thread of the argument in this section. The following overview and breakdown of Part 4 is offered in the hope that it will help the first-time reader to orient himself as he moves through the text. Following a brief excursus on the topic of freedom and bondage, our analysis will then follow the order of this overview.

READING THE TEXT

After an interesting account of the origins of the words 'perfect', 'imperfect', 'good' and 'bad', Spinoza offers a definition that ties these normative terms to an individual's power and success in the endeavour to persevere in being (Preface). He then devotes a few propositions to the subject of human beings' weaknesses and limitations (4p2–6) and to the means by which various passive emotions might be countered by the force of other emotions (4p1 and 4p7–18). The next propositions establish that the individual's conatic endeavour is the touchstone for judging good and bad and the foundation of virtue (4p19–25). In a crucial, interesting and controversial step, Spinoza then identifies that which is conducive to our perseverance in being with that which is conducive to reason and understanding (4p26–28). This somewhat changed perspective allows Spinoza to argue that nothing is more valuable to human beings than other reasonable human beings, and to sketch out a contract theory of the origins of the state based on this insight (4p29–40). Employing his own criteria, Spinoza examines a number of emotions to ascertain whether they are good or bad and asks, regarding certain character traits, if they should be counted as virtues (4p41–66). The account of the actions and emotions of an ideally virtuous person is rounded out with a description of 'the free man' (4p67–73). Finally, in a lengthy Appendix, Spinoza provides a summary of the contents of Part 4 rearranged in a more perspicuous order.

A preliminary note on freedom and bondage, activity and passivity

The titles of Parts 4 and 5 make reference to 'bondage' and to 'freedom'. This is a little surprising, for the reader has, until now, heard very little about freedom or the lack thereof. Spinoza has been quite forthright in insisting that there is no such thing as 'free will' – neither in us nor in God. That much is completely clear. But the reader might have forgotten that in d7 of Part 1 Spinoza offered a different definition of freedom. According to that definition to be free is to be self-determining – to 'exist solely from the necessity of [one's] nature and to be determined to action by [oneself] alone'. As we noted in the discussion of 1p17c2 only God can be truly free in this sense, for only he fully satisfies these criteria. But this definition leaves the door open for human beings to be free to some extent, for what we do is sometimes, to some extent, determined by ourselves.

The interest in human freedom helps to explain why the

distinction between 'active' and 'passive' is so important for Spinoza. We *act* – i.e. we are active – whenever something takes place (internally or externally) of which we are the adequate cause (3d2). We are the adequate cause of something when it can be understood as following from our nature or essence – i.e. from our conatic endeavour to persevere in being. But when we are the adequate cause of something, we can say that it is determined by us, and hence that we are acting freely. So it turns out, in Spinoza's view, that to the extent that we are active (as he understands that term), we are free (as he understands that term), whereas to the extent that we are passive (acted upon) we are unfree (in 'bondage'). This turns out to be central to Spinoza's argument.

We have seen already what Spinoza means when he says that we are often passive. Most of the affects discussed in Part 3 are passive affects (passions) caused in us when we are affected by things around us. To the extent that our emotions are produced in this way we are, in a sense, hostage to fate. Sometimes we will be fortunate – the things around us will strengthen us and make us happy. Often they will not. But in either case we are not in control of our emotional lives, and given that our behaviour is influenced by our emotions, we are thus not in control of our behaviour. We are, rather, passive. Things are not being determined solely by us – so we are, to that extent, unfree. We do have a kind of power with which to take some control and assert ourselves against the onslaught of these externally caused affects. This is the previously mentioned 'power to act' – the power with which each of us endeavours to persevere in being. But very often (indeed, most of the time) the affect-inducing external influences are stronger than our power to act, and we are not in control of our feelings, our emotions or our behaviour. On the contrary, our passions are in control of us, while we have little understanding of them and often are not even aware of their influence. This is the state of affairs that Spinoza refers to when he speaks of our being 'tossed about by the waves and driven by contrary winds'. In such a state we are emphatically not self-determining in our feelings and behaviours. Spinoza does not hesitate to call this state 'bondage'.

READING THE TEXT

Study question

1. According to Spinoza, to the extent that we are active, we are free. Explain how he arrives at that view.

Preface to Part 4 – On perfection and imperfection, good and evil
As he begins to address the basic questions of normative ethics, Spinoza pauses to explain his understanding of some basic evaluative terms. He contends that we say of some human artefact that it is 'perfect' if we think that it measures up entirely to the plans and intentions of the artisan who produced it. We declare it 'perfect' by comparing it with what was intended. If it fails to measure up, we call it imperfect.

Spinoza's point is even clearer in the original Latin, for the basic meaning of the word *perfectus* is 'completed'. (It is the past participle of the verb *perficere* – 'to complete'). The idea is that if the maker of something has not yet brought his work to completion, the item is imperfect – in both senses of the term.

Of course if we are unable to discern what the maker's intentions were or what purpose the artefact was designed to serve, then we are unable to say whether and to what extent it is perfect. With familiar items, though, we form our own notions of what they are supposed to be like – our own ideal models of various types of thing – and we readily pronounce things perfect or imperfect according to whether they measure up to our preconceived ideal. Then we extend this kind of evaluation to things in nature that are not human artefacts at all. If we see some natural object that does not live up to our preconceived ideal of that type of thing, we think that '... Nature has failed or blundered and has left that thing imperfect. So we see that men are in the habit of calling natural phenomena perfect or imperfect from their own preconceptions...'

According to Spinoza it is quite understandable that we should have fallen into this way of thinking, but it is nonetheless entirely wrong-headed, for it falsely assumes that nature, like a human artisan, has intentions or purposes in bringing things into being. We learned in Part 1 (especially the Appendix to Part 1) that God/nature acts for no purpose and has no ends in mind. On the contrary, all things follow from God with the same timeless, effortless and purposeless necessity with which it follows from the nature of a triangle that its angles equal 180 degrees. Human beings have desires, and we form intentions and act for the purpose of satisfying those desires. But our erroneous belief that nature acts with intention or purpose is just a result of our confused tendency to anthropomorphize. Once we realize that nature acts with no purpose or plan, we can see that our attribution of perfection or imperfection to natural objects is a confused projection based on our own made-up preconceptions of ideal types. Nothing in nature is objectively perfect or imperfect in itself, for there is no objective standard (Platonic forms or divine intentions, or whatever) by which to make the assessment. Spinoza concludes that 'Perfection and imperfection, therefore, are only modes of thinking, i.e. notions we are accustomed to feign because we compare individuals of the same species or genus to each other...'

Likewise the words 'good' and 'bad', '... indicate nothing positive in things, considered in themselves, nor are they anything other than modes of thinking ...' As in the case of perfection and imperfection, to say that something is either good or bad is to compare it with some notion that we have of an ideal model of that type. Our judgements of goodness and badness will thus always be relative to some such standard that we have devised. This is not in itself problematic, though problems arise when we mistakenly come to think that these qualities '... indicate something positive in things, considered in themselves'.

Spinoza knows that in the course of history different cultures, religions and philosophers have proposed differing ideals as touchstones for human goodness or perfection. As an ethical theorist Spinoza can hardly do without judgements of good and bad, and he has no desire to dispense with the concepts entirely. But he is methodologically self-conscious and wants to be careful about how he employs these concepts and about the standard that he proposes for making such evaluative judgements. So he explicitly says that '... we desire to form an idea of man, as a model of human nature that we may look to'. Having then formed an idea of such a model of human nature, we will be able to judge emotions, actions and institutions as good or bad. Indeed, Spinoza explicitly defines how he will be using the terms good, bad, perfect and imperfect by reference to this ideal model of human nature:

> So in what follows I shall mean by 'good' that which we certainly know to be the means for our approaching nearer to the model

of human nature that we set before ourselves, and by 'bad' that which we certainly know prevents us from reproducing the said model. Again, we shall say that men are more perfect or less perfect in so far as they are nearer to or farther from this model. (Preface)

Spinoza is quite open about the fact that he is making up this model of human nature that will serve as the basis for evaluative judgements. The model is just a mode of thinking – something that we feign. But it will become clear as we proceed through Part 4 that Spinoza does not believe that his model of an ideal human nature is arbitrary or that it is without a kind of objective foundation in nature. On the contrary, he believes – and will demonstrate – that his model of human nature reflects the fundamental endeavour to persevere in being that constitutes the essence of every individual. Spinoza thinks that the tie between his ideal model and the individual's conatic endeavour provides a kind of objective grounding for his ethical program. Looking ahead, we can foresee that in Spinoza's view what is good for an individual is what is conducive to greater power, activity, joy and freedom. The careful reader will notice that given Spinoza's definitions of activity, joy and freedom, these will all follow directly from an increase in power to act. But in order to achieve this greater degree of activity and freedom we must find a way to control and moderate the misleading and excessive passions.

Study questions

1. Is Spinoza right in his account of the origins of our use of the terms 'perfect' and 'imperfect'?
2. Spinoza says that we must have in mind an ideal model of human nature if we are to make evaluative judgements of good and bad, perfect and imperfect. This would suggest that every ethical theory or ethical doctrine that distinguishes good and bad must (at least implicitly) presuppose such a model. Is Spinoza correct about this?

The power of nature (and of the passions); the weakness of human beings (4p2–6)

We human beings are not self-caused. On the contrary, we are modes of the one substance, caused to exist and to act by other modes and by the laws of nature. We are dependent on food, water, air and other environmental conditions in order to survive at all. We can be debilitated and snuffed out by diseases, disasters, weapons and wars. We are in a constant struggle to persevere in a complex environment of supportive and destructive influences.

An individual's power to act can thus be positively or adversely affected by environmental influences of all kinds. To the extent that these changes result from external influences, the individual is by definition passive in this process. As we learned in Part 3, emotions are increases and decreases in an individual's power to act, and those emotions that we call passions are those that are caused by external factors.

Spinoza reminds us forcefully and repeatedly that an individual's status as a tiny part of the natural order ensures that his or her power is miniscule in comparison with the rest of nature. Thus we will always be affected in positive and negative ways by external things and always be subject to the passions. The one axiom of Part 4 makes these points, and propositions 2, 3, 4, 4c and 6 reiterate them in slightly different ways.

Countering emotions with other emotions; akrasia (4p1 & 4p7–18)

An emotion, so far as it is related to the body, is a transition – up or down – in the body's power to act. If I am being affected by pain or sadness my power to act is being reduced. To counter or to do away with that sadness requires that my level of power be raised – i.e. that there be a transition in the opposite direction – an increase in my power to act. But an increase in my power is by definition an emotion of joy. So in order to counter an emotion, a contrary emotion that is stronger than the first is required (4p7). And the same argument can be made on the mental side, for the mental aspect of these emotions is just the mind's affirmation that these transitions in the body's power of acting are taking place (4p7c).

Spinoza began to make the case for this claim in the very first proposition of Part 4 where he reminded the reader of an important result of the discussion of the imagination back in Part 2. Using one of his favourite examples, he reminds the reader that even when we learn the truth about how far away the sun is, our imaginational idea (our visual perception) will not be changed just by the fact that this information is newly acquired and is true. The sun will still appear to us as if it were 200 feet away, for this appearance is not positively false, to be dispelled by the truth. Rather, it is a true (albeit partial and limited) idea of how our bodies are affected by the sun. Changing this imaginational idea would require literally changing the way in which our bodies are affected – thereby dispelling the initial imaginational idea and countering it with another.

Spinoza's claim that affects can be countered only by other (stronger) affects provides him with a way of dealing with one of the oldest and most puzzling issues in moral psychology – the problem that the Greeks referred to as *akrasia*. In English this topic is usually called the problem of 'weak will' (though of course Spinoza would not like the phrase, for he denies the existence of the faculty of will).

Whatever term one uses, the psychological phenomenon in question is puzzling. Normally we assume that when we make choices we deliberate and then choose that option which we judge to be best for us. But any reluctant smoker or unsuccessful dieter knows that we can sometimes carefully weigh the options, judge one option to be clearly better for us, and nonetheless do the opposite. So I might judge that abstaining from smoking a cigarette is the best course of action, and nonetheless find myself lighting up. Or I might conscientiously judge that the damage done to me by continuing a relationship with a particular ladyfriend far outweighs the momentary pleasures of her company, and yet nonetheless ask her to join me for a holiday. For anyone who thinks of human beings as rational agents, cases of this sort are quite puzzling.

Reflection on this problem goes way back. Some (Socrates, for example) have denied that we ever do knowingly choose what is bad for us. Others have claimed that while in such cases we may have some superficial belief about what is good, we do not have fully fledged knowledge. Spinoza does not take either of these approaches. He grants that we do sometimes deliberately choose what we know to be the worse alternative – indeed he quotes Ovid as that poet sums up the akratic quandary, 'I see the better course and approve it, but I pursue the worse course.' And he allows that at the moment we make the akratic choice we can very well possess true knowledge of good and bad. Spinoza can make sense of the situation by reference to two characteristic aspects of his view that are the focus of this section of Part 4 – his account of just what knowledge of good and bad is, and his theory of competing affects.

In an initially surprising proposition Spinoza announces that 'Knowledge of good and evil is nothing other than the emotion of pleasure or pain insofar as we are conscious of it' (4p8). Upon reflection, though, this makes good sense on his terms, for that which is good is that which enhances my power to act, and pleasure is precisely an enhancement of that power. So, if something increases our power to act, we experience pleasure and desire to be further affected by that thing, calling it good. To be conscious of that process is to have knowledge of good and evil (4p8dem). But of course there may be other affective processes underway in us as well. For example, I may have desires, brought about by past experiences, associations, superficial similarities, etc., which lead me in a different direction – and I may be quite unaware of the provenance or indeed of the existence of those other affective processes. In such cases there will be conflicting affects within me, and it is entirely possible that the stronger one – the one that ultimately manifests itself in the action that I take – will not be the one reflected in my conscious 'knowledge of good and evil'. Note that in such a case (in Spinoza's terminology) I have not *acted*, for things that are contrary to my perseverance in being cannot follow from my conatic endeavour. Rather, I have been acted upon by the passion (the passive emotion).

Based on his earlier discussion of the dynamics of the imagination (in Part 2), Spinoza offers some interesting and plausible generalizations about what sorts of affects are likely to be stronger, and what sorts weaker. For example, the earlier discussion yields the conclusion that (other things being equal) the image of a future thing is feebler than the image of a present thing. Consequently, the emotion toward a present thing will be stronger than the emotion toward a future thing (4p9c). This would help to explain how the desire associated with my knowledge of good and evil with regard to smoking (which knowledge is my conscious pleasure in the image of my future health and avoidance of disease) would be outweighed by the desire produced by the promise of the immediate pleasure coming from the cigarette and the relief from the pains of nicotine withdrawal (4p17). Not surprisingly Spinoza shows that (other things being equal) emotions related to things that we know to be certain to happen are stronger than those related to things that we think might happen (4p11). After summing up a number of these generalizations about the relative power of various emotions, Spinoza concludes, in a series of three propositions (4p15, 16 & 17), that desires arising from a true knowledge of good and evil can often be outweighed and overcome by the power of other passive emotions. Thus Spinoza offers his solution to the traditional problem of *akrasia*.

Spinoza makes one more important point in discussing the relative strengths of different affects. 4p18 states that 'Desire arising from pleasure is, other things being equal, stronger than desire arising from pain.' This is Spinoza's more sophisticated version of the claim that the carrot is more effective than the stick – an important insight that Spinoza immediately puts to use. As an ethicist, Spinoza wants to encourage us to live a certain kind of life. Since he has established that a mere knowledge that that life is the truly good life is not enough to ensure that we actually adopt that path, he has to consider how best to induce us to do so. In principle he could dwell on the pain and confusion that attend a life of vice, and thereby influence us to want to avoid such a life (3p13). But since a desire that springs from pleasure is stronger than one arising from pain, Spinoza chooses instead to depict the pleasure and strength that attend a life of virtue, knowing that that will influence us to want to live such a life (3p12). And the desire kindled in us will be stronger in the latter case than in the former. The last section of Part 4, in which we learn of the life of the free man, is precisely an attempt on Spinoza's part to move us with the power of imagined pleasure to strongly desire such a life for ourselves.

In the Scholium to 4p18 Spinoza pauses for a moment to take stock of where we are and to inform the reader of where the argument is headed. He seems to realize that he is covering a lot of ground and that the reader may be missing the forest while contemplating the trees. It is a good, clear summary, and should be read with care in order to provide orientation as we go forward.

Study questions

1. On what basis does Spinoza claim that knowledge of good and evil is just joy (pleasure) and sadness (pain) in so far as we are conscious of these?

2. Why is *akrasia* a problem? How does Spinoza's account of competing emotions offer a solution to the problem?

Conatus as the foundation of virtue and the touchstone of good and evil (4p19–22 & 25)

Every individual endeavours to persevere in being (3p6) and in doing so seeks pleasurable things (that he judges good) and avoids painful ones (that he judges evil) (4p19dem). This endeavour just is the individual's conatic essence or nature. The more he succeeds in this endeavour, the more power he manifests. Spinoza identifies the individual's power with his virtue (4d8) and concludes that the more an individual succeeds in the endeavour to persevere, the more he is endowed with virtue (4p20). The Scholium to 4p20 reminds us that according to Spinoza's theory if a person fails to persevere in being (his example is a suicide) it can only be because he was weak and overcome by external factors. (We discussed this Scholium above – pp. 97–8, where we considered possible objections to 3p6.)

These claims about conatus and power, pleasure and pain, good and bad are all familiar by this point, but Spinoza reiterates and emphasizes them here as he starts to develop his own normative ethical views. Since everyone is motivated by the desire to survive, an ethical programme will be accepted only if it appeals directly to each person's self-interest. Spinoza is a clear-eyed egoist on this point. The only motives anyone has are self-interested motives, and it makes no sense to recommend an ethical doctrine on any other grounds. Of course people may not understand themselves adequately and they may fail to recognize what is truly in their self-interest. But the only appeal that will engage them motivationally is an appeal to their interest in maximizing their power to act (i. e. to survive).

The term 'virtue' (*virtus*) entered the Latin philosophical vocabulary as a translation of the Greek word *arête*, which can also be translated as 'excellence'. The Greeks often discussed what character traits make for human excellence, devising rich and interesting accounts of such presumably excellent traits as courage, wisdom and justice. In Roman times, (among the Stoics, for example), virtue came to be associated more closely with strength or fortitude of soul. Spinoza's position is closer to that of the Stoics, of course, but his point here is that both naturally and motivationally the power to persevere in being is prior to the moral excellence of Greek *arête*. In order to be wise, courageous or just, one must first exist (4p21). And since the endeavour to persevere in being is our essential and most fundamental source of motivation, this conatus must be the primary basis of virtue (4p22cor). As we saw above, in the discussion of the Preface to Part 4, Spinoza's ideal model of human nature, which will serve as a touchstone for judging good and bad, will be a model of maximal power for perseverance in being.

Power, virtue and the centrality of reason (4p23, 24 & 26–28)

In the midst of arguing that the endeavour to preserve oneself is absolutely fundamental, Spinoza reminds us of a point that he made way back at the beginning of Part 3. Using his definitions of 'adequate cause' and of 'acting', he argued that the mind can only be said to act insofar as it has adequate ideas. (See the discussion above at p. 90) To have adequate ideas (of which Spinoza's main examples are the common notions – see above, pp. 77–8), and to understand things in light of those adequate ideas, is to engage in reasoning, or the second kind of knowledge. To know things in this way is to understand things truly. So – we are really active only to the extent that we understand and are living under the guidance of reason (4p23 & 24). Propositions 4p26 and 27 go one step further, arguing that the only things that we know certainly to be good are those things that are conducive to understanding, while the only things we know with certainty to be bad are those that can prevent us from understanding.

The step that Spinoza takes in these few propositions is one of the most important conceptual moves in the entire system. He is identifying what is conducive to perseverance in being with what is conducive to understanding. In effect he is equating the endeavour to persevere in being – which he has declared to be the actual essence of the individual – with the endeavour to understand. Of course many thinkers have argued that human beings are essentially rational creatures, and that what is definitive of us (individually and collectively) is our capacity to reason and to understand. But until this point Spinoza's theory seemed different – he was more biologically focused, with emphasis on homeostasis, organic integrity and survival. Now it no longer seems that the mind mainly endeavours to affirm the body's continued existence and its power to act. Rather, the mind endeavours to reason and to understand.

A number of commentators have found this step questionable. Even if one agrees that the inference makes formal sense in light of the definitions of 'adequate cause' and 'act' offered back in Part 3, it remains unclear why the endeavour to survive as an organism should be identical with the endeavour to reason and understand. Granted, understanding is itself a pleasurable activity, and we therefore naturally desire it and judge it good. But that is not enough to warrant the claim that it is the only thing that we certainly know to be good. Of course we can think of various common-sensical ways in which it is advantageous for an individual and for the species to exercise reason and to understand. It is true, for example, that on the whole (other things being equal) a reasonable and knowledgeable person will have a better chance of living a long life than an ignoramus. Fools, after all, often die young. A rational person is more likely to be a reliable judge of what is conducive to survival and joy. And rational understanding has led to technologies (medical and agricultural technologies, for example) that have had the effect of prolonging human life.

In these ways it is clear that reason and understanding do tend to lead to greater power for self-preservation. Spinoza would no doubt welcome the mention of these examples. But he is making a more fundamental claim than can be justified by familiar facts such as these. Ultimately he is claiming not only that understanding is conducive to the highest good. He is claiming that understanding *is* the highest good. He makes this clearer in 4p28 when he says that 'Knowledge of God is the mind's greatest good; its greatest virtue is to know God.' It is understandable that knowledge of God would be the highest kind of knowledge and God would be the ultimate object of understanding. But it is not so obvious that knowledge or understanding (of God or of anything else) is the highest good of a being whose chief object of endeavour has already been shown to be perseverance in being.

In much of the remainder of Part 4 Spinoza will be using, as a criterion for judging things good or bad, the test of whether they are conducive to understanding or not. He will judge emotion and actions good or not based on whether they 'arise from reason' or are the sorts of actions that one would perform 'from the guidance of reason'. In Part 5 he will explain how reason can be brought to bear directly on the unruly and destructive passions, and how it can help to moderate their excesses, even transforming some of these passions into active emotions. Finally, we will see how, by achieving a rational understanding of ourselves as part of nature, we can alter our very conception of ourselves in ways that take us beyond questions of self-preservation. In these ways Spinoza will show the value and desirability of reason and rational understanding. So even if one is dubious about the derivation of 4p26 and 4p27 at this point, one may be convinced in the end. We will return to this pivotal question at the very end of our study.

Study questions

1. How does the earlier claim – that the mind acts only insofar as it has adequate ideas – support Spinoza's claim that the only thing we know to be good is understanding?
2. Suppose a thrill-seeker responded to Spinoza by explaining that her greatest joy/pleasure comes in sky diving, and hence that skydiving is that which she knows most certainly to be good. How might Spinoza try to convince this person that understanding is really the way to go?

Social life and the origins of the state (4p29–40)

Thus far Spinoza has not had very much to say about our interactions with other people – a subject central to most treatises on ethics these days. We have learned something about the ways in which attitudes and behaviours towards others can result from certain emotions and how the actions of others can affect us emotionally. But as yet there has been very little mention of the sorts of interactions with others that would be appropriate and desirable for an individual who pursues virtue under the guidance of reason. Spinoza seeks to fill that gap in a series of claims beginning with 4p29.

The deductive details of the first five or six propositions are not very convincing, but the general point that Spinoza is trying to make is clear enough. He wants to distinguish between those ways in which human beings all 'agree in nature' and those ways in which people are (or at least can be) 'contrary to' one another. Nothing can be destructive of us through what it has in common with us (or it would be destructive to itself, which is impossible) (4p30). On the contrary, so far as it agrees with us in nature it has to be good for us (since of course it must be good for itself) (4p31). So the more a thing agrees with us in nature, the better it is for us (4p31cor).

Spinoza then argues that to the extent that human beings are subject to the passions, they do not agree in nature. After all, the passions reflect the natures of the myriad things in the world that are affecting us more than they reflect our own nature. And those myriad things are all different and they affect us in different ways so that our passions differ (a point that Spinoza made back in 3p56). So to the extent that people are 'torn by affects which are passions' they can disagree in nature and can be contrary to one another (4p33 & 34). Spinoza uses the examples of accidental antipathy and jealousy as instances of the way passion-torn people can come to be contrary to one another (4p34dem).

But according to Spinoza insofar as people are active – that is, insofar as they act from virtue under the guidance of reason – they must always agree with one another (4p35). For if they are indeed under the guidance of reason, they will pursue that which is truly good for their human nature. And what is good for their own human nature will be in agreement with the nature of every person. Hence all those who live according to the guidance of reason will agree in nature (4p35dem). And finally, since the more a thing agrees with us in nature, the better it is for us (4p31cor), we can conclude that there is nothing in the universe more advantageous to us than another human being who lives by the guidance of reason (4p35cor).

In truth, this line of argumentation does not fare well when subjected to careful logical scrutiny. But the conclusion is plausible enough, and in the Scholium to 4p35 we are offered more down-to-earth reasons for accepting this conclusion. Spinoza points out that as things are now people seldom live under the guidance of reason and are very often a source of trouble and annoyance for each other. And yet even in these circumstances almost no one chooses to live a solitary life, and most people seem to agree with Aristotle's and Seneca's definition of man as a 'social animal'. We do clearly gain more from cooperation and fellowship with others than we lose.

> So let the satirists laugh as much as they like at human affairs, let the theologians curse them, let melancholics praise as much as they can a life that is uncultivated and wild ... Men still find by

experience that by helping one another they can provide themselves much more easily with the things they require ... (4p35s)

Spinoza notes that the highest good for a person who seeks virtue under the guidance of reason is common to all and can be enjoyed by all equally – it is the knowledge of God (4p36). This is important, for if the highest good were (in contemporary terminology) a 'zero-sum good' – i.e. if it were such that my having more of it required that someone else have less of it – then it would engender competition and put the virtue-seeking person at odds with his or her fellows. But not only is that highest good not a zero-sum good. On the contrary, the virtuous person has every reason to want others to have and enjoy this good also (in order that all may agree in nature, to their mutual support) (4p37). This presumably explains why Spinoza made the effort to write the *Ethics*. He wants to encourage others to seek virtue, to live under the guidance of reason and to enjoy the highest good.

In a second Scholium to 4p37 Spinoza offers a capsule version of his theory of the origin of the state – a theory developed much more fully in the *Theological-Political Treatise* and in the (unfinished) *Political Treatise*. Spinoza's views are heavily influenced by the work of Thomas Hobbes (1588–1679), an important British political theorist. Hobbes's theory envisions a 'state of nature', prior to the formation of a state, in which there are no civil laws and no authority to enforce agreements. Hobbes suggests that fear would motivate everyone to be suspicious of all others and to try, through violence, subterfuge or alliance with others, to maximize his or her power for self-protection. The state of nature would be a fearsome and nasty war of all against all.

Spinoza does not emphasize as graphically as Hobbes the violence and backwardness that would characterize this natural condition, but he knows well that people in the state of nature would be led by their passions and would be at odds with each other. Spinoza claims, too, that in the absence of any civil law every individual would, by 'the sovereign natural right', do whatever seemed to him advantageous to himself, would judge good and bad according to his own lights and would 'endeavour to preserve what he loves and to destroy what he hates'. If everyone lived by the guidance of reason there would be no problem (since all would recognize the great benefit of cooperation and would trust others to do likewise), but since most people are not virtuous and rational, there will be conflicts. Although they want and need each other's help, they will be at odds.

What is needed is a way for these people to come together cooperatively, working in harmony. In order to achieve that, each individual must be willing to give up her sovereign right to do whatever she wants and all must agree to refrain from harming one another. But how can all parties to this agreement be confident that it will be honoured by everyone? An enforcement mechanism is needed, and, since it has been established that a passion can be overcome only by a stronger contrary passion, the enforcement mechanism must be empowered to provoke strong fear by threat of punishment. This means I can trust my fellows to adhere to our mutual non-aggression pact if I know that they are cowed into cooperative submission by threat of punishment. 'Now such a society, strengthened by law and by the capacity to preserve itself, is called a State, and those who are protected by its rights are called Citizens.'

Spinoza emphasizes that in the 'state of nature', prior to the establishment of the civil state, there is no established criterion of good or evil, and hence that 'wrongdoing cannot be conceived'. Moreover, prior to the establishment of the state there is no property, and hence there can be no robbery. Indeed, there can be no justice or injustice of any kind prior to the agreement that brings into being both the state and the agreed-upon shared standards of justice.

The discussion of the state in the *Ethics* is very brief – so much so that the reader could get the impression that Spinoza does not think that the state or the political realm is very important. This would be a seriously mistaken impression. He gives scant attention to political issues in the *Ethics* because he has devoted two other works specifically to the subject. Being a citizen of a well-governed state is not by itself a sufficient condition for achieving human blessedness, according to Spinoza. But in a world such as ours, in which most people are ruled not by reason but by their emotions, the state is absolutely necessary to enforce, through threat and fear, some measure of cooperative interaction and mutual support among people. Hobbes famously says that in the state of nature there would be no culture of the earth, no commodious building, no arts, no letters, no society, and that the life of man would be 'solitary, poor, nasty, brutish and short'. Spinoza's view does not differ so very much from this Hobbesian assessment. The state is what saves most of us from that sort of miserable existence, and it is for that reason extremely important.

Study questions

1. Spinoza says that in a 'state of nature' everyone would do whatever he deemed to be advantageous to himself – and would do so 'by sovereign natural right'. What do you suppose this last phrase means?
2. Spinoza holds that prior to the establishment of the state 'wrongdoing cannot be conceived.' Why is that? Does Spinoza's view entail that all standards of right and wrong are a matter of convention?

Evaluating various emotions and actions (4p41–66)

Nearing the end of Part 4, with much of the moral psychology and normative theory in place, Spinoza applies the principles that he has derived to evaluate specific actions and emotions. He provides a more concrete sense, finally, of what the best human life would involve.

First he reiterates his earlier standard of goodness, reminding us that whatever is conducive to the preservation of the ratio of motion and rest among the parts of the human body is thereby conducive to the body's perseverance in being and will bring joy or pleasure – and is therefore good. If something undermines or destroys the ratio of motion and rest that is definitive of the body, it is therefore bad.

Spinoza takes this opportunity to discuss briefly the vexed question of whether an individual can cease to be the individual that she is prior to literal death. He thinks that it is possible for the ratio of motion and rest that is definitive of a person to change while that body nonetheless keeps breathing and living. In such circumstances, if the changed ratio of motion and rest is sufficiently different we can say that the individual has become a different person. As he rather graphically puts it, '... nothing compels me to maintain that the body does not die unless it is changed into a corpse'. Spinoza cites the example of a certain Spanish poet who suffered amnesia as a result of an illness and could not recognize his own writings as his.

If there has been such a significant change in the poet's memory, then there must have been (according to Spinoza's parallelism/identity theory) a significant bodily change as well. Spinoza seems prepared to admit that the amnesic poet is not the same man that he was. He mentions, too, that an infant and the later grown adult hardly seem similar enough to warrant the judgment that they are the same person. These are issues that are still hotly debated today, but having broached them Spinoza leaves them again in order to return to his main task of outlining the affective and behavioural contours of the good life.

Those things which are conducive to our increased power to act are good. Now that we know how valuable it is to live in harmonious cooperation with others, Spinoza can confidently say that things that are conducive to that kind of cooperation are good. Using these criteria he goes back through a number of emotions that were defined and discussed in Part 3 and judges them as good or bad. Joy, for example, is by definition good (and sadness naturally bad). That specific kind of joy/pleasure that is localized in only one part of the body (called *titillatio*) can, if excessive, undermine the body's healthy balance and render it incapable of enjoying other joys. Thus, titillation can be excessive and hence bad (4p43). Furthermore, the love and desire that arise from *titillatio* can also be excessive, as we see in the instance of someone so enamoured of his new lover that he cannot think or dream or talk about anything else. Spinoza puts this kind of obsessed lover in the same category as the greedy lover of money or the ambitious person obsessed by the desire for fame. In all of these cases, Spinoza does not hesitate to call it a kind of madness (4p44s).

Tucked into the Scholium to 4p45 is a poignant passage in which we find Spinoza praising the goodness and value of simple harmless pleasures:

> ...it is the part of a wise man to make use of things and to take pleasure in them as far as he can (but not to the point of satiety, for that is not taking pleasure). It is, I repeat, the part of a wise man to refresh and invigorate himself in moderation with good food and drink, as also with perfumes, with the beauty of blossoming plants, with dress, music, sporting activities, theatre and the like, in which each man can indulge without harm, to another. For the human body is composed of many parts of

various kinds which are continually in need of fresh and varied nourishment so that the entire body may be equally capable of all the functions that follow from its own nature, and consequently that the mind may be equally capable of simultaneously understanding many things.

This follows quite clearly from Spinoza's account of the body and the emotions, and it reflects his appreciation for the variety of nature and of the pleasures available to us. But it is poignant because it is hard to imagine Spinoza himself – impecunious, inclined toward solitude and not leaving his room for days at a time – dressing up, going to the theatre or engaging in sport.

In celebrating these pleasures *as* pleasures Spinoza is also striking a quiet blow against those dour theologians and those religious enthusiasts of his day who were suspicious of laughter, happiness and pleasure. This group might include many Calvinists as well as members of other Protestant sects (such as the Puritans) who urged a sober and drab virtue. The praise of a life of varied enjoyments is implicitly (and not so subtly) a critique of these people. And in case anyone missed the point, Spinoza says in this context, '... nothing but grim and gloomy superstition forbids enjoyment'.

For the next twenty-five propositions Spinoza applies his criterion for good and bad to various emotions and character traits, weighing whether they tend to increase one's power to act. Sometimes he finds that he can embrace the perspective of traditional Christian morality, and sometimes he must oppose it. For example, since hatred and the emotions that arise from hatred can never be good (4p45), a person who lives by the guidance of reason will respond to others' hatred with love. One might hear in that an echo of Jesus' command that we love even our enemies. On the other hand, humility is usually looked upon as a virtue in the tradition, whereas Spinoza explicitly denies this (4p53). Likewise, many might hold that repentance is a good thing, but Spinoza counsels against it, for '... he who repents of his action is doubly unhappy or weak' (4p54).

Humility and repentance provide good examples for noting the subtlety and the realism of Spinoza's position. These two emotions are not good, and the person who lives in accordance with reason would dispense with them. But in truth, very few people do live entirely in accordance with reason, and so these two emotions can serve the good purpose of checking our irrational tendencies in the opposite direction. Humility and repentance are not good, but they are much better than, say, arrogance and shamelessness, for they are less likely to bring us into conflict with others, and less likely to render us deaf to the appeals of reason. So – if we can avoid the whole lot of these emotions, all the better. But if not, better to err in the direction of humility and repentance. And this is presumably the reason that the prophets have been so adamant in urging these as virtues.

Following up on this line of argument, Spinoza concludes his evaluation of these various emotions by making an important point. Sometimes we can be moved to do something – something positive and good – by passive emotions that are not, in themselves, good. The most obvious example would be the fear of punishment that motivates many citizens to obey the law. Fear is a bad emotion, but it moves the citizen to do a good thing – viz. obey the law. It is of course better that we obey the law than disobey the law, even if we are being determined to obedience by a passive and painful emotion. But it would of course be better yet if we could be determined to obey the law without that painful emotion. Spinoza argues that since obedience to the law is truly good – i.e. it is conducive to our perseverance in being – we can be moved to do it by reason alone. Indeed, using 'action' in his technical sense, Spinoza makes the important claim that *any* action to which we can be moved by a passive emotion, we can also be determined by reason without the emotion (4p59).

Desires engendered by passions can be excessive; desires engendered by reason cannot (4p60 & 4p61). Desires arising from passions will be stronger for present gratifications than for future ones, even if the future gratification is better for us; desires arising from reason are not temporally skewed in this way (4p62s). Under the influence of passions – especially fear – we may shun evil; but under the guidance of reason we can arrive at the same result more reliably by pursuing the greater good or the lesser evil directly. Given that nothing good can arise from the passions that cannot arise from reason, and given that the passions can be problematic in all these ways, a wise and virtuous person will seek to minimize the role played by passive emotions in his life (to the extent that that is possible). This does *not* mean that he will try to live without emotions at all. On the contrary, his will be a life characterized by joy,

READING THE TEXT

love and the other active emotions that can arise from one's own power, that cannot lead one astray and do not give rise to greed, lust, envy, regret, remorse, vacillation, internal conflict or other emotions that have pain or sadness at their very core.

Study questions

1. Spinoza's vision of the good life is one of joy and pleasure, strength and activity. And yet he cautions against excess and against certain kinds of pleasures. Why are certain pleasures to be approached with caution?
2. Why is remorse a bad emotion (according to Spinoza)?
3. Is Spinoza correct in his assessments of which emotions are good and which are bad?

The free man

The virtuous person who lives thus under the guidance of reason, maximizing active emotions of joy and minimizing the passions, is freer than the individual who is tossed about on the waves of his passions. What he feels and what he does is self-determined, following from his own conatus – his own power to act. None of us will ever fully live this life, for we remain immersed in and dependent on things outside ourselves. Still, near the end of Part 4 Spinoza provides a little more information about the life of the ideally free person. Perhaps this is the 'ideal model of human nature' that he spoke of as he was defining his use of the terms 'good' and 'bad' back in the Preface to this Part.

4p67 tells us that 'A free man thinks of death least of all things, and his wisdom is a meditation of life, not of death.' In part this follows easily from the corollary to 4p63 which tells us that when our desires arise from reason we directly pursue the good rather than being guided by a fear and avoidance of the bad. Spinoza holds that the thought of one's death is necessarily a painful thought, likely to induce fear, and that a free person will have no need for such thoughts. On the contrary, he will find joy in the contemplation of his strength and life.

In a very important (and in some ways surprising) proposition (4p72) Spinoza claims that 'A free man always acts honestly, not deceptively.' In a Scholium to this proposition he asks the question that would naturally suggest itself to the reader. 'Suppose someone now asks: what if a man could save himself from the present danger of death by treachery? Would not the principle of preserving his own being recommend, without qualification, that he be treacherous?' In a response that sounds remarkably like the later German philosopher, Kant, Spinoza replies, 'If reason should recommend [treachery], it would recommend it to all men. And so reason would recommend ... that men make agreements, join forces and have common rights only by deception – i.e. that they have no common rights. This is absurd.' It seems as if Spinoza's identification of the individual's power to act with the adequate ideas of reason has led him away from the individual human organism's struggle for survival.[13] Of course he is dealing with 'the free man' at this point, but it is not clear just how a free man could be under present threat of death. To consider one's own demise would seem to induce passive emotions of fear, thus undermining one's status as a free man. Perhaps this will become clearer when we consider the power that reason can have over the passions (in Part 5).

Concluding Part 4

Spinoza has covered a lot of ground in Part 4, and he knows that the order of exposition and the connections among the topics may not always have been entirely transparent. In an effort to clarify and to reinforce the points made, he offers an appendix that sums up the doctrine of virtue and power, with an emphasis on the centrality of sharing life with others. No significant additional doctrines are introduced, but it is helpful and a pleasure to read through the ideas in a different arrangement and without the distraction of derivations and demonstrations. The Stoic element comes through in a beautifully expressed passage that serves as an appropriate transition to the final part of the *Ethics*: '... insofar as we understand we can want nothing except what is necessary, nor absolutely be satisfied with anything except what is true. Hence, insofar as we understand these things rightly, the striving of the better part of us agrees with the order of the whole of nature.'

PART 5 – ON THE POWER OF THE INTELLECT, OR ON HUMAN FREEDOM

As we read the closing words of Part 4 it might seem as if Spinoza has done what he set out to do. He has provided an account of our motives and passions, how they come to be, how we can be in bondage to them and how they can undermine human virtue. We have been told what is truly good for us and which of our emotions and ways of acting are conducive to that good. And Spinoza has provided a model of a virtuous person – for our inspiration and emulation – in his depiction of 'the free man'. It might seem as if he has explained what one needs to know to understand the good life for a human being.

But in the opening paragraph of Part 5 we learn that Spinoza has more to offer than the normative and descriptive account of the good life that we just finished reading. It turns out that he will also point out and explain 'the method or way leading to freedom'. He has in mind a method, based on 'the power of reason', by means of which one can liberate oneself from the bondage of the excessive and irrational passions. In one sense it is natural that Spinoza's method for addressing the passions would rely on 'the power of reason', for the mind's power to act consists in its having adequate ideas, and having adequate ideas is what comprises the 'second kind of knowledge, or reason'. On the other hand, it is a little surprising to hear him speaking of the passions being 'checked and controlled' by the power of reason, since he has made it clear that an emotion can only be checked by another, contrary emotion. The first half of Part 5 will clear this up by explaining how reason can exert power over the unruly passions.

Spinoza also mentions in this first paragraph, almost in passing, that he will explain '... what is freedom of mind, or blessedness, from which we will see how much to be preferred is the life of the wise man to the life of the ignorant man'. Again, we might think that we have already learned about 'the free man' and seen how his life is a model of peace, emotional stability and power to act and to persevere. But it turns out that the kind of freedom Spinoza has in mind is something much more remarkable even than this. Spinoza will explain how, by means of a kind of intuitive understanding of oneself in God, one can achieve blessedness (*beatitudo*). These are dramatic claims that have given rise to the suggestion that there is a kind of mystical element in this aspect of Spinoza's thought. These are also difficult and controversial doctrines that have resisted interpretation and provoked strong criticism from commentators. Spinoza, of course, purports to deduce them step-by-step with his usual logical certainty. We shall see what we can make of this blessedness.

Preface

Since he will be discussing the power that the mind can have over the unruly passions (and over the self-destructive behaviours that often result from these passions), Spinoza begins with a brief discussion of the views of others on this subject. He notes that the Stoics seem to have thought that we could control our emotions through a direct exercise of will – though they granted that it could be very difficult and could require extensive training and practice. Descartes, on the other hand, had an elaborate theory according to which an easily movable gland in the brain, called the pineal gland, can be moved by an act of the soul's will, and this gland's motion can, in turn, produce the motions of the animal spirits that yield desirable emotions and quiet unruly ones.

Spinoza of course rejects these views entirely. For one thing, they both presuppose the existence of a faculty of will – and Spinoza directly denies that there is such a thing. Moreover, Descartes' view presupposes that a volitional act of the non-physical soul can set a physical object – the pineal gland – in motion. How this can happen is left entirely mysterious in Descartes' system, and Spinoza takes him to task for it. 'Indeed, I am lost in wonder that a philosopher who had ... so often censured the Scholastics for seeking to explain obscurities through occult qualities, should adopt a theory more occult than any occult quality.' It is a sign of the deep respect that Spinoza had for Descartes – as well as the preeminent position that Descartes held in the scientific/scholarly world in the mid seventeenth century – that the pineal gland theory, with all its obvious difficulties, gets the one-page critical treatment that Spinoza gives it here.

Rational therapy for the passions

Spinoza cannot rely on the power of the will to help control the unruly emotions, for there is no will. The mind's power lies in its ability to understand – to gain (become) adequate ideas which affirm the order of things as they truly are, as they follow from the infinite power and activity of God. The order of things as presented in adequate ideas differs markedly from the order of things as affirmed in the imagination, for the latter order reflects only the order of interaction of the body with other modes – an order necessarily eccentric given the particular nature, place and perspective of the individual body. We imagine things as contingent or possible; we know them as necessary. We imagine things as durational; we know them under an aspect of eternity. We imagine things as separate inert particulars; we know them as various ways in which the unitary and divine substance acts. Spinoza claims that the attainment of an adequate conception of nature, ourselves and our emotions will qualitatively change those emotions, making them subject to us (insofar as this is possible) rather than our being subject to them.

The first half of Part 5 explains how rational understanding can have these salutary therapeutic effects. This explanation, in turn, is developed in three stages. First (5p1–4) Spinoza provides a somewhat abstract account of the effect of our gaining an adequate understanding of a particular emotion. This account is couched in the technical terminology of the system, and while the logical connections can be followed pretty easily, the experiential meaning is not entirely clear. Fortunately, the next series of propositions (5p5–10) provides a series of 'remedies' for the unruly passions that are intuitively plausible and can be understood in everyday experiential terms. These too depend on our gaining an adequate understanding of things, but the affective import of that understanding is more easily grasped. In the final group of propositions of the first half of Part 5 (5p11–20) Spinoza notes that the more we understand the more we will love God. That love will necessarily be a strong love and will have other characteristics that make it especially valuable for assuaging the power of the bad emotions. A lengthy Scholium after 5p20 summarizes these 'remedies' and provides a transition to the final account of human blessedness.

Gaining adequate understanding of the emotions (5p1–4)

In the first proposition of this Part Spinoza reminds the reader of the parallelism/identity of the two known attributes. The order and connection of affections of the body are the same as the order and connections of the ideas thereof. This ensures that any conclusion we draw regarding ideas in the mind will be reflected in parallel facts occurring in the body (and vice versa).

The next proposition (5p2) reads as follows: 'If we remove ... an emotion from the thought of its external cause, and join it to other thoughts, then love or hatred toward the external cause, and also vacillations that arise from these emotions, will be destroyed.' The proof, while clear enough in its own way, is frustratingly abstract.

Since love and hate are defined as joy or sadness accompanied by the idea of an external cause, if the idea of the external cause is removed, there will (by definition) no longer be love or hate toward that cause. Formally speaking, this makes sense. But what exactly does it mean to 'remove' (*amoveamus*) an emotion from one thought and to 'join' (*jungamus*) it to other thoughts? And though the love or hate might no longer be there, the joy and sadness presumably will be. So how is this an improvement in one's situation?

Looking ahead to 5p3 we find Spinoza talking about forming a clear and distinct idea of a passive emotion. In 5p4 he emphasizes that there is no affection of the body of which we cannot form a clear and distinct idea. So the 'removing' and 'joining' of emotions and ideas seems to be related to our forming a clear and distinct idea – gaining an adequate understanding – of the emotion. In light of our discussion of Spinoza's theory of the first and second kinds of knowledge in Part 2, we can say that to remove the emotion from the idea of an external cause is to cease imagining the emotion (according to the common order of nature) to be the result of the external cause (of which one has at best a confused idea anyway). To unite it with other thoughts is then to understand it as following from ideas of the ways in which God always and everywhere acts (i.e. the common notions).

This process can best be understood by returning to Spinoza's example of our idea of the sun. Insofar as I cognize the sun only according to the common order of nature, my idea of the sun is in fact (unbeknownst to me) an idea of the way my body is affected by the sun – an idea which, in light of various confused associations in my imagination, suggests that the sun is about 200 feet away from me. Insofar as I attain to adequate ideas of perspective, geometry, optics and the human sensory apparatus, however, my idea can be seen to follow from these as exactly what it is – viz. an idea of a modification of my body, which modification is caused (in accordance with the laws of nature) by a vast ball of energy more than 93 million miles away. In this case my idea has been removed from the various ideas associated with it in the imagination and 'joined' to other more adequate ideas from which it follows more clearly and distinctly. So too in 5p2 above – the idea of the emotion must be removed from the thought of the external cause and united with those ideas from which it follows more clearly and distinctly. Since the pleasure or pain is then no longer accompanied by the former idea of the external cause, the love or hate of that imagined cause is gone.

The next step is outlined in 5p3 where we are told that 'A passive emotion ceases to be a passive emotion as soon as we form a clear and distinct idea of it.' Spinoza's demonstration of this is hard to interpret, but the proposition seems to follow easily enough given his definitions. Given that the idea of the emotion follows from ideas that are adequate in the mind, these ideas in the mind can be said to be the adequate causes of the idea of the emotion, and hence the mind can be said to be active *vis à vis* that idea. Thus, simply by coming to understand a passive emotion we cease to be passive with regard to it. As if to emphasize that this must be seen as a matter of degree, Spinoza goes on to conclude, '... the more an emotion is known to us, the more it is within our control, and the mind is less passive with respect to it'.

These propositions follow reasonably well, in their own terms, but difficult questions remain unanswered. For example, when Spinoza urges that we form a clear and distinct idea of an emotion, should we understand this to mean specific *occurrences* of an emotion or *types* of emotions? Although he doesn't make it clear, presumably he means both, for knowing about the typology of emotions and the etiology of each type is essential for understanding a specific instance of an emotion of that type. If one is suddenly overcome with anger toward an individual, one can more readily understand that specific onslaught of anger if one knows, generally, what anger is and why it occurs.

A more serious interpretive difficulty arises if we reflect on the very nature of the recommendation that Spinoza is making. He is recommending that we overcome destructive, sadness-related emotions through acquiring an adequate understanding of them. The problem is that according to Spinoza's doctrine it is impossible, in principle, for us to gain an adequate understanding of sadness. Sadness is, by definition, a transition to a state of lesser power and perfection. If we could gain an adequate knowledge of sadness, it would have to be the case that the idea of a transition to a lower state of power could follow from ideas adequate in our minds. If this were the case, our minds alone would be the adequate cause of this idea of a transition to a state of lesser power. But this is impossible, for nothing can follow from our minds alone except ideas of that which is conducive to our perseverance in being – and ideas of transitions to states of lesser power and perfection are not conducive to our perseverance in being. It seems, then, that Spinoza is recommending the impossible.

The best response to this objection is to accept it – not as a damaging problem but as a confirmation of the efficacy of understanding in overcoming sadness and sadness-related emotions. Just as it follows that pain cannot be understood, so too it follows that that which is adequately understood cannot be pain. But while this makes sense in formal Spinozistic terms, it would be nice to have a more experiential grasp of the points he is making. For that we have to turn to the next group of propositions.

Study questions

1. If we were to come to the sort of understanding of a painful emotion that Spinoza recommends regarding our imaginational perception of the Sun, would it change the character of the emotion? Why or why not?
2. What difficulty is there in the notion that we can form a clear and distinct idea of a painful emotion?
3. Is it true (as Spinoza says), that '... the more an emotion is known to us, the more it is within our control, and the mind is less passive with respect to it'?

Specific cognitive remedies for the passions (5p5–10)

We want to understand, in less formal and more experiential terms, just how passive emotions are transformed as we gain an understanding of them. In propositions 5p5–10 we find a series of claims about how our emotional response to something will be different if we know it as it truly is. All of these claims are psychologically plausible and experientially familiar.

For example, 5p5 tells us that (other things being equal) we will have the strongest emotional response to something that we simply imagine as present – rather than thinking of it as necessary, or possible, or contingent. 5p6 claims, in turn, that we have greater power over the affects insofar as we conceive of things as necessary. Since all things and events in nature are in fact necessary, if we conceive of things as they truly are we will conceive of them as necessary. So Spinoza holds that if we conceive of things as they truly are, our emotional responses will be less strong and we will thus have greater power over them. But why does he think that thinking of things as governed by necessity will weaken their affective hold on us?

The proof and Scholium of 5p6 are interesting in terms of the variety of psychological insights they offer. For example, Spinoza argues that if I simply imagine something, without any relation to its causes, I am in effect imagining it to be uncaused or self-determining – i.e. I am thinking of it as if it were free. Spinoza deduced back in Part 3 (3p49) that our emotional response would be strongest towards something that we imagine as free (in this sense). He reasoned that the love or hatred of a thing lessens when the joy or sadness caused by that thing is associated not only with that thing, but with other causes as well. The idea is that love or hatred can be (so to speak) 'diluted' by enlarging our conception of the causes of the joy or sadness involved therein. Thus, emotion towards any single thing is lessened when we consider the causes of its being as it is (doing as it does). When we know a thing truly and adequately, then, our emotion towards it will lessen significantly, for it will be diluted by consideration of the innumerable other things that are causally efficacious in having brought about our joy or sadness. Thus, we will be more able to control such emotions in order that they not become excessive or destructive.

It might be objected at this point that the emotion is still there even when we achieve an adequate understanding of its cause. After all, the joy or sadness is still as great, and is still 'accompanied by the idea of an external cause' (definition of love and hate). But instead of hating the thundercloud that just flooded out his field, the farmer now hates the entire universe! This objection has some merit, but it can be answered within Spinoza's psychological system. As the purview of the emotionally affected person fans out to encompass more and more of the causes of the specific object of the emotion, prior and different affective associations with various of these other causes will assert themselves, some (perhaps most) of which will work against the power of the original emotion in question. Furthermore, eventually this purview must include (in the given example) the farmer himself and finally God. But the farmer does not, presumably, hate himself, and for reasons to be discussed below, he cannot hate God. On balance, then, his hatred will indeed be ameliorated.

It is interesting to note that this dilution strategy, though it is found in the proof to 5p6, does not really turn directly on the *necessity* of the object of the emotion. The Scholium to 5p6, however, does give examples, based on experience, of more direct ways in which we can see the connection between necessity and lessened emotion. The first example reads as follows: '... we see that the pain over the loss of some good is assuaged as soon as the man who has lost it realizes that the good could not, in any way, have been saved'. This is a familiar sort of experience, and it illustrates nicely a way in which the recognition of necessity can ameliorate emotional reaction. But it does not depend on the dilution of the emotion via recognition of multiplicity of causes. Contemporary psychologists might explain the phenomenon in a different way. Part of the pain and sadness suffered upon the loss of some good is a matter of regret, self-reproach and perhaps guilt at not having prevented the loss. One feels that one ought to have done something, but failed to do so, and this sense of failure brings about some of the sadness. Thus the pain can be lessened by the recognition that '[the good] could not, in any way, have been saved'. Nothing one could have done would have changed the course of events, so one has no reason for feeling remorse or guilt at one's failure, and that part of the sadness that derived from the remorse or guilt is reduced.

One is reminded here of Epictetus' recommendation that we be constantly mindful of the distinction between those things that are within our power and those that are not. According to the views of this Stoic, the contemplation of the fact that many things simply are not within our power can be used not only as a *post hoc* remedy for excessive emotional disturbance, but also as preventive medicine to strengthen the mind against upsetting passions. If we are sufficiently mindful of what is and what is not within our power we can, with sufficient effort, limit our wants and desires in such a way that we will not suffer the pain of frustration at unfulfilled expectation. Spinoza would agree with Epictetus here, differing only in the fact that on his view it is not a matter of exerting 'effort' to control our emotions. In Spinoza's view the adequate ideas of what is and what is not within our power would themselves entail the negation of the ideas of our having and accomplishing things that are beyond our power, and would thus weaken the latter as images and hence as imaginative objects of desire. As he states in the final paragraph of the Appendix to Part 4, '... insofar as we understand, we can desire nothing but that which is necessary...'

The mention of Epictetus is appropriate, too, to the second example that Spinoza offers as experiential confirmation of views. He notes that no one pities a baby even though infants are unable to speak, walk or reason, and barely seem fully conscious. 'But if most people were born adults, and only a few were born babies, then everyone would feel sorry for babies because they would then look on infancy not as a natural and necessary thing but as a fault or flaw in Nature.' (Remember – pity is not a good emotion, so Spinoza counts it a gain if we do not experience pity.) This is another good example of Spinoza's overall point, but again it does not seem to depend on the dilution of the affect through cognition of multiple causes. The psychological mechanism seems, rather, to be related to the recognition that infancy is a natural and necessary state in the human developmental process. Of course for Spinoza every event is in fact natural and necessary, and if we only know things truly we will know them as such and be less susceptible to emotional upset regarding them.

It should be noted that Spinoza does not claim that adequate cognition and recognition of necessity will completely and permanently do away with all excessive emotions or irrational desires. The best mathematician, in times of poverty, may well desire that it be the case that a quarter and a dime equal five dollars. He might even (conceivably) be angry that they do not. But his anger and desire *vis à vis* the mathematical facts of the matter will not overwhelm him.

In the Scholium to Proposition 10 Spinoza offers a helpful discussion of the limits of these remedies, but also of their impressive power. If we know how the emotions arise and if we are mindful of which are good and which are bad, and of which actions are conducive to our power and virtue (and which are not), we will be fortified to maintain self-control when we encounter situations that otherwise might provoke excessive or unruly emotional response. We can give ourselves rules of conduct, and rehearse in our minds the sorts of circumstances in which these rules should be applied – so that when such circumstances actually do arise the association established in our minds will ensure that these rules will be readily available for service. And of course we can seek to know things as they truly are – i.e as they follow necessarily from the divine nature, caused by an endless series of causes that proceed in accordance with the law-like ways in which God/nature always and everywhere acts.

Study questions

1. The ancient Taoist sage Chuang Tzu makes an interesting point about the emotions. He says that if we are in a small boat on a river and an empty boat floats down the river and runs into our boat, we will not fly into a great rage. But if there is a person in that other boat, we will shout and admonish and get quite angry. The presence of a person in the other boat makes the difference in our emotional irritability. What Spinozistic principle (or principles) does this Taoist lesson illustrate?
2. How does the 'dilution' strategy work to lessen our emotional responses?
3. Are Epictetus and Spinoza correct in thinking that we are less susceptible to emotions of sorrow or pity regarding some adverse event or circumstance if we consider the event or circumstance to be 'natural and necessary'?
4. Will we in fact have more control over our passions (and be less controlled by our passions) if we keep the outlines of Spinoza's therapeutic programme in mind?

Understanding and the love of God (5p11–20)

In 5p4 we learned that there is no affection of the body – no image and no emotion – of which the mind cannot form a clear and distinct idea. This means that there is no affection of the body of which we cannot attain an adequate conception. But to know something in this way is to know it as it follows from God. Thus, there is no affection of the body which cannot be related to the idea of God (5p14). Not only is it related to God – it is known to follow from God.

To come to know oneself and one's emotions in this way is to experience an increase in one's power and virtue – i.e. to experience joy. And this joy is accompanied by the idea of God as its cause. Thus (by definition) one loves God (5p15). And this love is always available (so to speak) for one's every image and emotion can be understood in this way. Hence, this love, associated with all the affections of the body (all images and emotions) is bound to hold chief place in the mind (5p16). And it will be impossible for us to hate God, for to think of God is to have an adequate idea from which many things follow – i.e. to think of God is to be active and to experience joy rather than sadness. And without sadness there can be no hate.

Since there is nothing outside God that could affect him from without, he is without passive emotions. Since God cannot pass to a greater or a lesser state of power or perfection, he cannot experience joy or sadness (5p17). Hence, God cannot (strictly speaking) love or hate anyone, for love and hate presuppose joy and sadness (5p17c). Since God cannot love or hate, our love of God cannot be tainted with envy or jealousy. We cannot want God to love us more than others (or indeed to reciprocate our love at all), for to want that would be to want God not to be God – and as intelligent beings we do not want the impossible.

This is an inspiring doctrine. Spinoza claims that the more we know of nature and of ourselves as a part of nature, the more we will be empowered and feel joy. This joy in our own power of understanding is related always to God, and yields a free and unselfish love of God that is not grasping or insecure. This joyful love holds central place in the mind as painful passions and self-destructive desires lose their controlling grip on us as we come to understand them, too, as following in law-like ways from the power of God.

Note, too, that this doctrine of the love of God suggests an implicit criticism of the more anthropomorphic conceptions of God held by traditional religions. The Judaeo-Christian image of God as a divine judge and potentate encourages the believer to desire to be loved by God and to be jealous lest others be loved more. One is led to fear the divine wrath, to disdain the adherents of other sects, and to construct elaborate rituals to propitiate God's wrath and to curry his favour. Spinoza views all this as superstition, based on a fundamental misunderstanding of the nature of God. As a result of this misunderstanding the thought of God, which should be a source of strength, joy and love, is turned into an occasion for anxiety, fear, envy and jealousy.

The Scholium to Proposition 20 recaps the various ways in which the mind can achieve a measure of control over the passions. Spinoza reminds us that all of these ways depend, more or less directly, upon our coming to understand ourselves, our emotions and the things around us as these follow from God.

Quite unexpectedly, at the end of the Scholium, Spinoza says, '... now I have completed all that concerns this present life ... So it is now time to pass on to those matters that concern the duration of the mind without respect to the body.' With these words Spinoza introduces the final doctrine of the *Ethics* – the difficult and controversial doctrine of the eternity of the mind.

Study questions

1. Why does knowledge of things as they truly are lead to love of God?
2. Why can God not love us in return?

Eternity and blessedness (5p21–42)

The final propositions of Part 5 make up the least well understood section of the *Ethics*. Commentators have despaired of discerning what Spinoza means here, and one well-known critic has dismissed this section as an unmotivated and unmitigated disaster.[14] It is certainly an interpretive minefield, for reading one proposition in a specific way brings one into conflict with another proposition or with other basic Spinozistic doctrines. Yet alternative readings seem to fare no better. Interpreting all of the claims in a way that makes them consistent and intelligible has proved a formidable challenge.

There are two difficult doctrines in this final section of the work – a theory of the eternity of the mind and an account of the intellectual love of God. Part of the reason these doctrines have proved such a challenge to commentators is that they depend on three further tenets of Spinoza's system, all of which have been mentioned earlier, but none of which has been really clarified in detail. These three are intuitive knowledge, essences and eternity. Since they all play a role in these final doctrines of the *Ethics*, their respective unclarities reinforce each other, making it hard to pin down exactly what is being said. Before delving directly into the propositions that articulate the doctrines of the eternity of the mind and the intellectual love of God, we will look briefly at each of the three previously mentioned tenets, hoping to establish at least the outline of a reading that does justice to all three while making sense as a whole.

READING THE TEXT

The third kind of knowledge (intuition)

In Part 2 (2p40s), after recounting his theory of the imagination and after explaining the 'second kind of knowledge' (reason) that depends on the common notions, Spinoza mentions a third kind of knowledge that he calls 'intuition'. Very little is said about this kind of knowledge, but we are told that it '... proceeds from an adequate idea of the formal essence of certain attributes of God to an adequate knowledge of the essence of things'. This kind of knowledge begins and ends with adequate knowledge, so we can be confident that imagination has no role to play here. We will have occasion shortly to consider what is meant by the claim that it yields knowledge of the essence of things. But a prior question relates to just how this kind of knowledge differs from reason (the second kind of knowledge).

In the one example that Spinoza provides – a case of finding the fourth proportional when given a ratio and a third number – he suggests that when we are dealing with simple numbers, anyone can 'infer in one single intuition the fourth number from the ratio we see the first number bears to the second'. The phrase 'infer in one single intuition' brings to mind the way in which Descartes explained the difference between intuition and deduction in his account of the different ways of knowing. Deduction, he says, is a step-by-step process, requiring time, memory and a 'movement or succession' of the mind in which the reasoner moves through the steps of a deductive inferential chain, ensuring that the conclusions do indeed follow validly from the premises in question. Intuition, on the other hand, is an immediate inference in which one 'sees' in one instantaneous insight the logical connections and implications that lead from premises to conclusion – without the need to reason it out step-by-step in deductive fashion.[15]

Sometimes people say, in a metaphorical way, that in a valid deductive argument the conclusion is 'contained' in the premises. This means that nothing additional is needed in order to establish the truth of the conclusion – it is all already there, so to speak, in the premises. The reasoner must only unfold the implicit contents of what is there in the premises. So, too, it can be said (again metaphorically) that the conclusion contains the premises from which it follows. One who understands how the conclusion depends for its warrant on the claims made in the premises, recognizes those premises as providing the grounding for the conclusion.

Keeping these metaphorical claims in mind, if we read 'intuitive knowledge' along Cartesian lines, we can say that the person who has an intuitive understanding of a deductive argument can 'infer in a single intuition' the implicit presence of the conclusion in the premises and the premises in the conclusion. Spinoza likes to say that 'logical proofs are the eyes of the mind' (5p23s), and one could say that the person who has intuitive knowledge regarding some inference can 'see' (with the eye of the mind) the conclusion implicit in the premises and the premises manifest in the conclusion. And in this context we should remember that Spinoza understands causation along the lines of logical implication.

Returning to Spinoza's explicit definition of the third kind of knowledge, we can assume that when this kind of knowledge 'proceeds' from an adequate idea of an attribute to an adequate idea of the essence of things, it is proceeding inferential-deductively. But it is presumably performing this inference 'in one single intuition'. So – since the attribute is that which the intellect conceives of as constituting the essence or power of God (1d4) – intuitive knowledge sees the essence of things as implicit in God and following immediately from the power of God. Likewise, it sees the divine power implicitly present in the essence of things.

Study questions

1. How does intuition (knowledge of the third kind) differ from reason (knowledge of the second kind)?
2. Talk of 'seeing God in individual modes' and 'seeing individual modes as present in God' is metaphorical talk. How can we unpack these claims in less metaphorical ways?

Individual essences

In defining the third kind of knowledge Spinoza uses the phrase 'the essence of things' (with the word 'essence' in the singular). In the doctrine of the eternity of the mind, though, he writes as if individual things have individual essences (plural). In either case, though, the reader is left somewhat in the dark regarding exactly what is meant by 'the essence' or 'essences' of things. We know that in the case of God Spinoza identifies his essence with his power (1p34). In the case of individual things (simple or composite) he identifies the thing's essence with its conatic endeavour/tendency to persevere in being. How are we to understand what a thing's essence is?

We had occasion to discuss individual essences once before – in the context of a particularly difficult proposition in Part 2 (2p8 & c). Right after establishing the parallelism/identity between the modes of extension and the modes of thinking (2p7), Spinoza raised the problem of how to understand the status of things which do not exist at a given time. He argues that even if, at a specific time, some thing does not exist, nonetheless its essence is contained in the attributes of God. The example we used in discussing this proposition (not Spinoza's example) was the dinosaurs. Spinoza would say that the essences of the dinosaurs are contained in the attribute of extension, just as the ideas of those essences are contained in the attribute of thinking. Employing the model of the laws of nature – that describe the regular ways in which God always and everywhere acts – we interpreted Spinoza's claim to mean that the laws of nature entail (deductively) that when certain causal conditions obtain (climatic, genetic, geological, etc.) dinosaurs will exist. Even when those conditions are not being fulfilled, though, the essences are contained (timelessly) in the attribute of extension. Connecting this point more directly to Spinoza's discussion of individual composite modes of extension (such as ourselves) we can say that the laws of nature entail that under the right causal conditions a certain complex configuration of simple bodies will come together and will be characterized by a certain ratio of motion and rest among those parts, and that this composite body will tend to maintain its physical integrity (i.e. the ratio of motion and rest among its parts) as it interacts with other things in the environment. To say that the laws of nature entail that the individual will exist under certain causal conditions is to say that the essence of the individual is contained (timelessly) in the attribute of extension.

There is for each of us such an essence – contained (timelessly) in the attribute of extension. And of course there is an idea of that essence contained (timelessly) in the attribute of thinking. To have an intuitive (third kind of) knowledge of oneself would be to proceed, in one single intuitive insight, from an adequate knowledge of the attribute of extension to an adequate knowledge of the essence of one's body. One sees one's essence contained in the power of God, and one sees the power of God manifest in one's essence. It should be remembered here that to the extent that one is able to acquire such knowledge one's mind contains those adequate ideas – indeed, one's mind becomes, in part, these adequate ideas.

Eternity

Time (duration) and eternity are important concepts in Spinoza's metaphysical system, but he has maddeningly little to say about them. He is confident that his readers will all have a sense of what is meant by the term 'eternal' for he knows that his readers will have some acquaintance with mathematics (especially geometry) and logic. One of Spinoza's favorite examples of a truth is the fact that the angles of a triangle add up to 180 degrees. He says that this is an eternal truth, presumably in part because it is simply inappropriate to apply temporal terms to it. A person who remarks that this was true yesterday or that it will be true next week is not speaking falsely, but he is saying something inappropriate and even absurd. Time and temporal references have no place in relation to a geometrical truth such as this one.

This is a familiar and on the whole unproblematic notion of eternity. But Spinoza applies the term 'eternal' to much more than just simple geometrical theorems. We noted, in reading Part 1, that Spinoza holds that God and all of God's attributes are eternal. Everything that follows from the attributes does so with the same eternity and necessity that is characteristic of mathematical relations and logical implication. Specifically, the essences of things that are 'contained' in the attributes follow from the power of God eternally.

In discussing the second kind of knowledge, or 'reason', we found that when we know things in this way we know them 'under a certain form of eternity' (*sub quadam specie aeternitatis*). To know things by means of reason is to know things as they truly are. This would suggest that to know things as they truly are is to know them under the form of eternity. But if this is so – if knowing something truly is to know it under the form of eternity – what then are time and duration? Spinoza provides some guidance in the Scholium to 5p29:

> We conceive of things as actual in two ways: either insofar as we conceive them as related to a fixed time and place, or insofar as we conceive them to be contained in God and to follow from the divine necessity. Now the things that are conceived as true or real

in this second way, we conceive under a form of eternity, and their ideas involve the eternal and infinite essence of God...

It seems that actual things can be conceived (so to speak) under the form of time or under the form of eternity. To think of them under the form of time is to think of them as related to a fixed time and place. One is tempted to say that things can be conceived in this temporal way when the causal conditions specified in the thing's essence have actually been fulfilled and the entity in question (say, the composite extended body characterized by a certain ratio of motion and rest among its parts) has come into existence. This would be in the spirit of the discussion in 2p8cor, but it must be remembered that the fulfilment or non-fulfilment of these causal conditions is not a contingent matter. These, too, follow with necessity from God, and with the reintroduction of necessity comes the reintroduction of eternity. In short, the process whereby an essence comes to be instantiated in time can itself be known under the form of eternity, thus calling into question the status of the temporality.

This issue has been a source of difficulty for Spinoza scholars since the publication of the *Ethics*, and we will not be able to resolve it here. But our brief consideration of the third kind of knowledge, the doctrine of essences and the view of eternity should provide enough background to address the final propositions of the *Ethics*.

The idea of the essence of the body under the form of eternity

The proposition that initially puzzles the careful reader is 5p23: 'The human mind cannot be absolutely destroyed along with the body, but something of it remains, which is eternal.' At first blush it sounds as if Spinoza is hinting at some kind of mental life after death. The body is destroyed at death, but something of the mind remains. That would sound familiar to Christian readers who think in terms of the soul's immortality, but it cannot be what Spinoza has in mind, for it would be inconsistent with 2p7 – the parallelism/identity claim that is absolutely central to his entire philosophy.

The proof of 5p23 makes it clear that the 'something' of the mind that remains after the destruction of the body is the idea that expresses the essence of the body under the form of eternity. From our discussion above we know that the essence of the body does indeed follow eternally from the divine essence under the attribute of extension. And there would of course be an idea of that essence that would follow in the same way from the essence of God expressed through the attribute of thought. Given that both the essence of the body and the idea of that essence are contained timelessly in God, it is puzzling that Spinoza mentions only the idea and suggests (by saying nothing about the essence of the body) that only something of the mind 'remains'. In fact if there is an idea of the essence of the body there is also the essence of the body.

Perhaps Spinoza is trying to make a kind of concession to his more religiously traditional readers by focusing on the non-physical aspect here. But it seems a little odd that he should start being solicitous of the sensibilities of the traditional believer at this late stage in the *Ethics*. And in any case, the traditionalist who is reading carefully will not find much of what he is looking for in Spinoza's view, for in 5p21 we have been told that the mind can exercise neither imagination nor memory except while the body endures. This makes sense, given that the imagination and memory are all about the way in which the body is affected by other things. But if there is no memory and no imagination in the absence of the body, then anything mental that might remain after the death of the body would have no memory of having lived and would have none of the usual experiences that make up a normal person's (chiefly imaginational) mental life. In the absence of memory and imagination, the timeless existence of the idea of the essence of the body cannot really count as personal survival or immortality.

A number of commentators have asked why we should care that the idea of the essence of my body under the form of eternity is timelessly in God. The power of God understood through the attribute of extension – the ways in which God always and everywhere acts extendedly – timelessly entails that under the right conditions my body will exist. Why should this fact be of interest to me? The answer is not immediately obvious, but if we pay attention to the next few propositions we see that Spinoza thinks that the idea of the essence of the body has a role to play in our minds now (to use an unfortunately durational term). He claims (5p29) that the idea of the essence of the body underlies the mind's ability to know anything under a form of eternity. When we remember that it is characteristic of reason (the second kind of knowledge) to know things under a form of eternity, we can infer that the idea of the essence of the body underlies all of our rational understanding.

Study questions

1. The essence of my body and the idea of that essence follow timelessly from the eternal essence of God (under the respective attributes, extension and thought). Should I find comfort in that when I am feeling troubled by the durational demise of my body and mind?
2. According to Spinoza the part of my mind that is eternal is without imagination or memory. In what sense can it be said to be *me*?

Reason and the idea of the essence of the body

It is not immediately obvious why our reasoning should depend on the idea of the essence of the body, but a plausible (if somewhat speculative) account can be offered. Reasoning depends on the common notions – the ideas of that which is common to all things and equally in the whole and in the part of all things. We interpreted the common notions to be ideas of the ways in which God always and everywhere acts (above, p. 77–8). But how does the human mind gain access to these ideas? The mind is the idea of the body, and if the mind contains ideas of the ways God always and everywhere acts, it must be because the body contains these very ways in which God acts. 'Contains' is an odd word here, but it is surely true that these ways in which God acts are present in the body, for the body's existence and continuity depend on these very constancies – the constancies that we describe in terms of the 'laws of nature'. So my mind has access to (contains) the common notions as a result of the presence in my body of those ways in which God acts of which the common notions are ideas. But the specific constellation of these ways in which God acts that determines the conditions for the coming-into-being of my body is the essence of my body. Thus, to the extent that an individual's mind consists of the common notions, it consists of ideas of those things that jointly constitute the essence of that individual's body.

The more things a person knows by the second kind of knowledge, the more her mind consists of the common notions – which are in her mind because they are ideas of those things that constitute the essence of her body. They are ideas of the ways in which God acts – and as ideas of the essence of her body they reflect the fact that she follows from the power of God and she is in God and

God in her. In 5p30 we read that 'Our mind, insofar as it knows both itself and the body under a form of eternity, necessarily has a knowledge of God, and knows that it is in God and is conceived through God.'

To know that I am in God and conceived through God is to know how the essence of my body follows eternally from the power of God. This knowledge is best understood as deductive, for (to take Spinoza's favourite example) the essence of my body follows from the power of God as it follows from the nature of a triangle that its angles equal two right angles. In the Scholium to 5p23 we find the interesting claim that when the mind engages in deductive inference of this sort, '... we feel and experience that we are eternal'. Spinoza goes on to say that '... the mind senses those things that it conceives by its understanding'. While he does not elaborate on this claim, anyone who has engaged extensively in deductive reasoning (say, in mathematics or logic) knows of the feelings of timelessness and necessity that Spinoza is referring to.

Study questions

1. How is the essence of my body related to the ways in which God timelessly and everywhere acts extendedly? How is the idea of the essence of my body under the form of eternity related to the common notions?
2. Spinoza would have us contemplate the timeless truths of the divine nature and the way in which we are timelessly contained in that nature. He claims that in doing so we can 'feel and experience' that we are eternal. Does that resonate with anything in your experience?

Intuitive knowledge (again)

We have already learned that to know oneself truly (by means of reason) is to know God and to know oneself to be in God. It is also to feel and experience that one is eternal. In the final propositions of the *Ethics* Spinoza invokes the third kind of knowledge – intuition – to boost the level of this knowledge and this experience yet further. In this kind of knowledge there is no need for the step-by-step deductive inference, for one can simply see, in one immediate insight, the inferential connections that lead from premises to conclusion. Any residual element of temporality drops out. To know something by means of intuitive knowledge is to see it, with the eye of the mind, in God – to see it as contained in – while following timelessly from – God and to see the divine power manifest in and as it. To know oneself in this way is to see oneself in God and to see God manifest in and as oneself. At this point one's mind consists chiefly of ideas of the common notions – a constellation of which constitute the idea of the essence of one's body. To know oneself in this way is directly to know oneself to be a part of and participant in the eternal activity of God or nature. This is the most powerful kind of knowledge, according to Spinoza, and it yields the highest possible contentment of mind (*acquiescentia animi*) (5p27).

The intellectual love of God (5p32–5p38)

The highest possible contentment of mind sounds like a positive emotional state, and Spinoza claims that from this positive emotion will arise love – specifically a love of God. Love is, after all, joy or pleasure accompanied by the idea of an external cause. But there is a problem with this claim – and Spinoza is well aware of it. Joy or pleasure is defined in terms of a transition to a higher level of perfection (above, p. 100). But a transition requires time and change, and we are talking here of a human mind that is eternal and recognizes itself as such. How could there be change (as required for joy/pleasure) in eternity? Spinoza responds:

> ...although we are at this point certain that the mind is eternal insofar as it conceives things under a form of eternity, yet, to facilitate the explanation and render more readily intelligible what I intend to demonstrate, we shall consider the mind as if it were now beginning to be and were now beginning to understand things under a form of eternity, as we have been doing up to now. Thus we may do without any danger of error, provided we are careful to reach no conclusion except from premises that are quite clear. (5p31s)

Spinoza holds that even though there is not change or transition in this high state of contentment, yet there can be positive enjoyment of perfection. 'If pleasure consists in a transition to a state of greater perfection, blessedness must surely consist in this, that the mind is endowed with perfection itself' (5p33s).

So the mind experiences the highest kind of contentment and blessedness, accompanied by the idea of God as the cause. Thus the mind experiences love of God. But this is an intellectual, rather than a passive love or a physical love. This intellectual love of God (*amor dei intellectualis*) is eternal (5p33) and without admixture of passive emotion (5p34). Spinoza suggests that God also loves himself with an intellectual love, and (in a passage reminiscent of Meister Eckhart or Nicholas of Cusa) claims that the mind's intellectual love towards God is the same love as the love with which God loves himself.

Study questions

1. Why is the doctrine of the intellectual love of God problematic in light of Spinoza's official definition of love?

Last things

These are inspiring and high-flying doctrines, but it is hard to know whether one has interpreted them correctly. In Proposition 38 we are brought back to earth with a claim that those who know things by the second and third kind of knowledge will suffer fewer bad emotions and, specifically, will be less likely to fear death. This is not because they are optimistic about the rewards that await them on the other side. Rather, the larger part of their minds is occupied with eternal ideas and hence not concerned with notions of duration. Many commentators have noted, too, that while Spinoza's doctrine of the eternity of the mind does not provide for personal immortality, it does relieve one of the fear that one will be made to suffer in the next world.

And with these considerations Spinoza returns from the discussion of the mind's eternity to remind us that understanding and the knowledge and love of God are our highest virtues. It seems that he is concerned that having addressed the question of what happens after death, he may have misled readers into traditional superstitious ways of thinking of the afterlife as a time of reward and punishment. In the final proposition of the *Ethics* he reminds the reader that virtue is its own reward, and that it would be foolish indeed to refuse to live the best life just because one will not be rewarded for it in another life. Or to choose to live a life of servitude, vacillation and sadness just because one will not be punished for it in the hereafter. Such attitudes are all too common, but they are unworthy of a thoughtful and rational person.

Spinoza wrote the last lines of the *Ethics* knowing that he might never see them in print. He knew that if the work were published the clergy would be hostile, the traditionalists fearful and most readers uncomprehending. And yet he spent more than ten years of his short life working on this most systematic of philosophical texts, pointing out the way to virtue. As he concluded he was mindful that he was writing not for the many, but for the few. The path to blessedness and salvation that he had outlined was steep and not likely to appeal to everyone. But in closing he admonishes us not to let that discourage us:

> If the road I have pointed out as leading to this goal seems very difficult, yet it can be found. Indeed what is so rarely discovered is bound to be hard. For if salvation were ready to hand and could be discovered without great toil, how could it be that it is almost universally neglected? All things excellent are as difficult as they are rare.

NOTES

1. Spinoza obviously intended the work to be read in the order in which he wrote it. But he realized that at times the geometrical method can be difficult to follow, and so he inserted, at intervals, scholia, appendices and prefaces written in less formal and more accessible language. The first-time reader of the *Ethics* might profit from a certain preparatory exercise before undertaking to read the full text. A good idea is to go through the entire work reading only the scholia, the Appendices (to Parts 1, 3 and 4) and the Prefaces (to Parts 3, 4 and 5). This can provide a more accessible orientation to the project and indicate the direction that the argument as a whole is going. With luck it will also whet the reader's appetite to learn more from the propositions and demonstrations.
2. From Galileo's 'The Assayer' in Stillman Drake, *Discoveries and Opinions of Galileo*. Garden City, NY: Doubleday Anchor Books, 1957, pp. 237–8.
3. From Lodewijk Meyer's 'Preface' to Spinoza's *Parts I and II of Rene Descartes' The Principles of Philosophy demonstrated in the geometric manner*. Trans. Samuel Shirley. Indianapolis: Hackett Publishing, (1998 – original 1663), p. 1.
4. Curley, E. M., *Spinoza's Metaphysics: An Essay in Interpretation*. Cambridge, MA: Cambridge University Press, 1969.

5. Letters 60 and 83 (both to Tschirnhaus).
6. Jonas, Hans (1973), 'Spinoza and the Theory of Organism', in Marjorie Grene (ed.), *Spinoza: A Collection of Critical Essays*. Garden City, NY: Doubleday/Anchor Press. pp. 259–78.
7. We are dealing here with error rather than evil, but the problem is in some ways analogous to the traditional 'problem of evil' in Judaeo-Christian terms. If God is all-good and He is the creator of all there is, how did evil come into being? To answer this difficulty by appeal to human 'free will' (or to Adam and Eve's free choice) is similar to Descartes' strategy. But as we noted, that path is not open to Spinoza.
8. We had occasion to mention this view above, in relation to Descartes' effort to explain how we make mistakes (p. 68).
9. An important contemporary neuro-scientist, Antonio Damasio, has recently written about his discovery of Spinoza's theory of the affects. Damasio asserts that in many important ways Spinoza had it right regarding the emotions and the role of the emotions in our cognitive and normative lives. See Antonio Damasio, *Looking for Spinoza*. Orlando: Harcourt, 2003.
10. Pollock and Della Rocca both appeal to these passages in the PPC when discussing the meaning of 'conatur' for Spinoza. See Frederick Pollock, *Spinoza: His Life and Philosophy*. London: Duckworth, 1899, p. 109 and Michael Della Rocca, 'Spinoza's metaphysical psychology', in Don Garrett (ed.), *Cambridge Companion to Spinoza*. Cambridge: Cambridge University Press, 1996, p. 196.
11. The following discussion summarizes ideas found in J. Thomas Cook, 'Der Conatus: Dreh- und Angelpunkt der Ethik', in M. Hampe and R. Schnepf (eds.), *Baruch de Spinoza: Ethik* (Volume 31 in the Klassiker Auslegen series). Berlin: Akademie Verlag, 2006, pp. 151–70.
12. I am following E. M. Curley's translation of 'tristitia' as 'sadness' and 'laetitia' as 'joy.' The reader should keep in mind that some translators have thought it more appropriate to translate these terms with 'pain' and 'pleasure' (respectively). There are good arguments to be made for both of these alternatives. The reader should just keep in mind that tristitia is a negative emotional state – an individual's transition to a lower degree of power to act. Laetitia, on the other hand, is a positive emotion – a transition to a higher level of power.
13. Don Garrett has an excellent critical analysis of this proposition and scholium in his 'A Free Man Always Acts Honestly, Not Deceptively': Freedom and the Good in Spinoza's *Ethics*', in E. Curley and P. F. Moreau (eds), *Spinoza: Issues and Directions*. Leiden: Brill, 1990, 221–38.
14. See Jonathan Bennett, *A Study of Spinoza's 'Ethics'*. Indianapolis: Hackett, 1986.
15. Rule 7 in Descartes' Rules for the Direction of the Mind, in G. E. M. Anscombe and P. Geach (eds), *Descartes: Philosophical Writings*. Indianapolis: Bobbs-Merrill, 1971.

CHAPTER 4

THE INFLUENCE OF THE *ETHICS*

Spinoza's greatest work, the *Ethics*, was published in early 1678 – a year after his death. As we saw in Chapter 1, the authorities made efforts to prevent its publication, but Spinoza's friends worked quickly and clandestinely to bring the *Opera Posthuma* to print in the original Latin and in a Dutch translation as well. As expected, within six months of its publication the work was prohibited in all of Holland and in other parts of Europe as well.

It is difficult to assess the influence of the *Ethics*, specifically, in the period directly following Spinoza's death, for his *Theological-Political Treatise*, published earlier (in 1670) was better known to readers of the time. We can, however, investigate the influence of Spinoza generally, and of the main ideas associated with his name – ideas that had already come to be called 'Spinozism'. Even here, though, it is difficult to be confident about the extent of the influence of these ideas, for Spinoza's works were still prohibited and one could be arrested and imprisoned, even in liberal Amsterdam, for openly advocating those of his ideas that were viewed as religiously and politically subversive. There were a number of published attempts to refute Spinoza's views (the views of the *Ethics* as well as those of the *Treatise*), but few writers dared openly to associate themselves with his ideas in a positive way.

SPINOZA'S CIRCLE, UNDERGROUND FREETHINKERS AND THE 'RADICAL ENLIGHTENMENT'

Still, there had been a circle of friends who respected Spinoza's thought and who got together to discuss his writings even during his lifetime. Some of these were the friends who prepared the *Ethics* for posthumous publication. In mostly informal ways, away from the eyes of the authorities, they continued to spread the seeds of Spinozism for some years after the master's death. On the one hand, there were those ideas, mostly from the *Treatise*, that were sharply critical of revealed religion and established religious institutions. On the other was the argument in the *Ethics* for an immanent God, a deterministic world and a naturalistically based ethic. These ideas were the subject of discussion among groups of freethinkers, and though they did not make it into the mainstream, they fed an underground current of radical thought in the late seventeenth century.

Intellectual historians have traditionally held that Spinoza's views had very little influence in the hundred years after his death. These views were, after all, highly unconventional and it was dangerous to be associated with them. In the minds of most thinkers and authors of the time, 'Spinozism' was a term of opprobrium – just another word for subversive atheism. But in a recent work of very impressive historical scholarship, Jonathan Israel has argued that Spinoza's ideas were very much alive in this period, spreading throughout Europe and helping to inspire a 'radical Enlightenment'. This movement, underground and yet widespread, was critical of revealed religion and ecclesiastical authority, and encouraged freedom of thought in matters relating to political authority, civil equality and even gender roles. Israel sees this 'radical Enlightenment' as extremely important in the development of the more familiar high French Enlightenment, and (more importantly) in building the intellectual foundations of modernity itself. As Israel says, '... a close reading of the primary materials strongly suggests, at least to me, that Spinoza and Spinozism were in fact the intellectual backbone of the European Radical Enlightenment everywhere, not only in the Netherlands, Germany, France, Italy and Scandinavia, but also Britain and Ireland'.[1]

G. W. LEIBNIZ AND PIERRE BAYLE

This movement may well have been, as Israel suggests, both historically important and deeply indebted to Spinoza. But it has remained to a great extent invisible, both in its own time and in historians' accounts of the period. Moreover (for our purposes) it is often not so easy to pin down specific traces of the '*Ethics*' in the writings of this group. But the situation is quite different with regard to two other philosophers associated with the name of Spinoza in the late seventeenth century – Leibniz and Bayle.

Gottfried Wilhelm von Leibniz (1646–1716) was a younger contemporary of Spinoza who developed his own complex and subtle metaphysical system over the course of a long lifetime's reflection. He too is normally classified as a rationalist, and he had a deep interest in many of the same metaphysical questions that occupied Spinoza. As a young man Leibniz instigated a correspondence with Spinoza about optics, hoping to draw the older philosopher into a more broad-ranging discussion of philosophical questions. In 1672, while living in Paris, he tried to learn more details of Spinoza's views from a colleague named Tschirnhaus who was a personal friend of Spinoza, had gained the latter's trust and possessed a manuscript copy of part of the as-yet-unpublished *Ethics*. A few years later (1676) Leibniz stopped in The Hague to pay Spinoza a visit in person, and they spent a few afternoons in conversation. It seems that what interested Leibniz about Spinoza was, in part, the fact that the two shared many assumptions, but that Spinoza's reading of the implications of these assumptions led to systematic conclusions that Leibniz very much wanted to avoid. Leibniz was a Christian, but he was acutely aware of the challenge to some versions of traditional Christian thinking posed by the new mechanistic 'natural philosophy'. He wanted to do justice to the achievements of this new approach to nature while holding on to the main tenets of the Christian faith.

Living in Hanover in 1678 Leibniz eagerly awaited the arrival of his copy of Spinoza's *Opera Posthuma* as soon as they were published. He devoured the *Ethics*, soon writing to a friend that he found it a mixture of 'beautiful thoughts', 'paradoxes' and some ideas that would be dangerous for some readers. Leibniz was never a Spinozist, but in various ways his metaphysical reflections took him dangerously close to the latter's radical views.[2] Later in his life, as he became increasingly devoted to his task of saving Christian dogma and the Christian mysteries from the onslaught of philosophical criticism, he was rather secretive about the extent of his earlier eager interest in the person and doctrines of Spinoza. Still, it seems that as he developed his philosophy he often cast a glance in the direction of Spinoza's *Ethics* to make sure that his own thought was not veering too close to the views of that notorious radical.[3]

Pierre Bayle, a French thinker living in Rotterdam, was one of the most widely read authors of the late seventeenth century. His works are still discussed, even today, for he writes in intriguingly enigmatic ways that make it difficult to interpret just what message he is ultimately trying to convey. Bayle's connection to Spinoza is twofold. First, he published a massive *Dictionnaire historique et critique* in 1697 that included a very long article on the life and thought of Spinoza. Ostensibly the article was intended to refute the paradoxical views of Spinoza, but its main result was to make Spinoza's system better known to thousands of readers who would not have attempted to read the *Ethics*. The second way that Bayle plays a role in the story of Spinoza's influence results from the biographical account that he offers in the *Dictionnaire* article as well as in an earlier work.[4] Spinoza is depicted as an atheist, to be sure, but a 'virtuous atheist'. There was a lively debate at the time about whether atheists could be tolerated in the community. The assumption on the part of many was that an atheist, not fearing punishment or hoping for reward in the afterlife, would be likely to commit crimes, to violate oaths, to bear false witness and thus to undermine public peace and order. Bayle uses Spinoza as an example of an atheist who lived a morally exemplary life and was a model citizen. This brought Spinoza to the attention of many, in a favourable light. To the extent that he came to be seen as the embodiment of a virtuous man who held unorthodox religious views, his very life was seen by some as an argument for toleration.

EARLY EIGHTEENTH CENTURY

In the early eighteenth century the *Theological-Political Treatise* continued to be much better known than the *Ethics*. The *Treatise* had been translated into Dutch, French and English, and had provoked innumerable refutations from all over. The *Ethics*, by contrast, existed only in Latin and Dutch, and though the original *Opera Posthuma* could be found in libraries in all parts of Europe, most people with knowledge of the content of the *Ethics* had garnered that knowledge from secondary sources, especially Bayle's *Dictionnaire*.

A few freethinkers in Great Britain, usually identified as deists, seem to have been influenced by the doctrines of the *Ethics*. One of these, John Toland, coined the term 'Pantheism' (in 1705) to refer to a doctrine, like that espoused in the *Ethics*, that identifies God with all of nature.[5] The term became a shorthand way of referring to Spinoza's metaphysical views, though like 'Spinozism' it was a term of dismissal and in the common mind, hardly distinguishable from atheism.

Another French thinker (other than Bayle) who was influenced by the *Ethics* and who made an important contribution to keeping Spinoza's ideas alive was Henri, Comte de Boulainvilliers. He seems to have been converted to Spinozism by studying the *Treatise* and then (in 1704) the *Ethics*. He went so far as to translate the *Ethics* into French for his own personal use (and that of a small circle of friends), though this translation was not published. He wrote a defence of Spinoza's system against the criticisms of the French philosopher Regis, and later composed an 'Essay de Métaphysique' in which he summarizes and presents the doctrine of the *Ethics* in a form less formidable than Spinoza's own geometrical exposition. The latter essay circulated in manuscript but was not published until 1731, nine years after Boulainvilliers' death. It appeared, together with some critical texts, in a volume entitled *Réfutation des erreurs de Benoit de Spinoza*. This work was very important in spreading and publicizing Spinoza's views throughout French-speaking Europe. Voltaire later quipped that in the *Refutation* Boulainvilliers 'gave the poison and forgot to give the antidote'.[6] Spinozistic ideas gradually found their way to the freethinking *philosophes* of the high French Enlightenment.

Aside from important conceptual parallels between Spinozism and the ideas of the French materialist La Mettrie or of the Encyclopediste Diderot, one can hear echoes of Spinoza in the confessions of the Savoyard vicar in Rousseau's *Emile*. Spinozistic ideas also found their way into politial discussions taking place across Europe and even in the United States. Although Locke was certainly the main direct source of political ideology for the American Revolution, Thomas Jefferson's personal library contained both of Spinoza's works – the *Theological-Political Treatise* and the *Opera Posthuma*.

In Germany at this time Spinoza's ideas were most often discussed in the context of the controversy surrounding the philosophy of Christian Wolff. Wolff was a professor in Halle who developed a systematic metaphysical position that looked, to his opponents, suspiciously similar to Spinozism. He was dismissed from his position by the king in 1723, went into exile, and continued to develop and defend his ideas. His views were in fact closer to Leibniz than to Spinoza, but the controversy was important, in part because the accusations against Wolff called attention to the positions of Spinoza and led to a more serious study of the texts. After two decades of exile, Wolff was called back to his position in Halle when a new king – Frederick the Great – ascended the throne.

In the midst of the controversy surrounding Wolff's exile, a translation of the first five books of the Bible was published (1735) – a work that came to be known as the 'Wertheim Bible'. The translator was a young man named Johann Lorenz Schmidt, and his translation was carefully crafted to remove all mention of the supernatural or miraculous from the text, as well as all mention of the ostensible Old Testament foretelling of the coming of Jesus. Wolff had been supportive of Schmidt, personally and professionally, and so suspicion was rife that the Wertheim Bible was a natural result of the Wolffian philosophy. Opponents did not fail to notice that this reading of the Pentateuch was the sort of thing that might be expected from one who is influenced by Spinoza's *Treatise* and its naturalistic biblical critique.

These opponents felt vindicated when, in 1744, Schmidt published his own German translation of the *Ethics*. It was bound together with a refutation of Spinoza's doctrines by Christian Wolff, but critics suspected that the inclusion of the refutation was just a smokescreen in order to get the *Ethics* published. The publication of Schmidt's translation was important, for it marked the first and only published translation of the *Ethics* into a European language since the Dutch version, which appeared simultaneously with the original *Opera Posthuma* sixty-six years earlier. The publication of Schmidt's translation can also be taken as an indication of the less stringent philosophical and theological censorship under Prussia's new 'enlightened monarch', Frederick the Great.[7] In Berlin there was, for the first time, open and quite extensive discussion of Spinoza's ideas in the newly revived Royal Academy of Sciences. Schmidt's translation of the *Ethics* was a careful and accurate work, and it served to introduce several generations of German scholars to Spinoza's system.

THE INFLUENCE OF THE *ETHICS*

THE PANTHEISM DISPUTE (*PANTHEISMUSSTREIT*)

Gotthold Ephraim Lessing (1729–1781) was a poet, dramatist, critic and highly regarded figure in the German Enlightenment. A proponent of religious tolerance and of freedom of thought, he worked these themes into his popular and now-classic works for the theatre. He was also a close friend and supporter of Moses Mendelssohn, a widely respected Jewish philosopher who held to his traditional faith while embracing a Leibnizian-Wolffian philosophy. After Lessing died, F. H. Jacobi, a philosopher and mutual friend, told Mendelssohn of a conversation that he had had with Lessing in 1780. Jacobi reported that Lessing had openly avowed that he (Lessing) was a Spinozist. Mendelssohn, who knew Spinoza's thought well but remained a more traditional Jewish believer, did not want his friend Lessing's memory tarred with the brush of Spinozistic pantheism. A correspondence, and eventually a well-publicized disagreement developed between Jacobi and Mendelssohn regarding what Lessing had believed and, more generally, about the implications of Spinoza's thought. Mendelssohn, though not a Spinozist, defended the role of reason in religion. Jacobi argued that reason could not get us to any God but Spinoza's, and since that is no real God at all, we must surpass reason in a leap of faith ('*salto mortale*'). Writers from all over took part and took sides. The upshot was a serious and open discussion of Spinoza's philosophy, pro and con, and the ultimate result was a thorough reassessment of his thought.

POETS AND IDEALISTS

Among the most enthusiastic of Spinoza's supporters was Goethe, the most important German writer of the period. In a couple of passages that have become well known, he expressed the feeling of sublime selflessness and clarity of vision that came over him as he read the *Opera Posthuma*. Goethe knew that his temperament was different from that of Spinoza, but found great value even in that contrast:

> The serene level of Spinoza stood out against my endeavor in all directions; his mathematical method was the complement of my poetical way of observation and description, and his formal

treatment, which some could not think appropriate to moral subjects, was just what made me learn from him with eagerness and admire him all the more.

Several members of the German Romantic movement embraced various aspects of Spinoza's philosophy. Most famously, perhaps, Novalis, an early Romantic poet (and a student of mysticism) reversed the verdict of generations of critics who had considered Spinoza an atheist. Novalis countered that, on the contrary, Spinoza was a 'God-intoxicated man'. In philosophy, the German Idealists after Kant were heavily influenced by Spinoza. Hegel and Schelling both wrote about Spinoza in an extremely positive way, the former famously saying that in order to be a philosopher one must first be a Spinozist: '... when one begins to philosophize, the soul must commence by bathing in this ether of the One Substance ...' Hegel did not accept Spinoza's position in the end, of course, but as a necessary starting point. From the perspective of his metaphysical idealism, he held that Spinoza's substance had to become self-conscious subject.

This re-evaluation of Spinoza's philosophy in the late eighteenth and early nineteenth centuries marks a remarkable change in his fortunes. Once viewed as a monstrous pariah whose ideas could be spoken only for purposes of refutation, he became recognized as one of the most important and admirable philosophers of the modern period. This re-evaluation began primarily in Germany, but it spread across the continent and into Great Britain as well. One of the most important figures in bringing the newly acceptable Spinoza to English-speaking lands was the poet, Samuel Taylor Coleridge. He brought Spinoza's thought to the attention of Wordsworth and others of the Romantic school. It is not a coincidence that the first enthusiasts for Spinoza at this time were the poets. Neither Coleridge nor Wordsworth, for example, accepted the details of Spinoza's philosophical system, but they were inspired by the identification of God and nature, intrigued by the daunting geometrical exposition and moved by the simple, virtuous and intellectually rich life of the philosopher.

The 1880s and 1890s brought a flurry of scholarly activity, especially in Britain. A number of commentaries and critiques were published, often by philosophers with Hegelian leanings who saw in Spinoza's substance an important predecessor of Hegel's Absolute

Spirit. In the Netherlands societies were formed to promote Spinoza studies, and to purchase and preserve two of the houses in which Spinoza lived.[8]

While Spinoza did not have a direct influence on Nietzsche, it is interesting to note that when the latter first encountered the *Ethics* he wrote an excited note to his friend Overbeck (1881) proclaiming that he had discovered that he had a forerunner, '... and what a forerunner!' It seems, on the other hand, that Sigmund Freud was influenced by his reading of Spinoza in the construction of the theory of unconscious emotions and in the belief in the therapeutic value of coming to understand the origins and etiology of these emotions.

RECENT DEVELOPMENTS

There were a few important philosophers who were influenced by Spinoza in the early and mid twentieth century (one might mention Bertrand Russell and George Santayana among English-speaking thinkers). It is notable, too, that there was quite a lot of active Spinoza scholarship in the Soviet Union, for Spinoza was looked upon as something of a materialist and as a worthy predecessor of Hegel and hence Marx.

The last few decades, however, have been the time of most dramatic growth in the amount and the quality of scholarship devoted to Spinoza's thought. In general, French scholars have focused their attention on the *Treatise* and on Spinoza's political views, while the Anglo-American world has focused chiefly on the *Ethics* and the metaphysical system. A number of national Spinoza societies have been formed (in France, the US, Germany, Spain, Italy and Japan) and an international journal, entitled *Studia Spinozana*, has been publishing since the 1980s.

In Britain and the US a number of factors have come together to prompt the rather dramatic upsurge in interest in Spinoza. For one, recent developments in computers and in brain science have contributed to an intense interest in the mind and how it is related to the brain – topics in a field called 'philosophy of mind'. Spinoza is of interest to scholars in this field because he had an entirely novel theory of how the mind and brain are related. Of course Spinoza's theory of the two attributes is not accepted by anyone today in just the way Spinoza developed it. But his view remains suggestive for those who think that ultimately what we call the mind will be understood as physical processes of the brain and body under a different description. In addition, at least one prominent neuroscientist thinks that Spinoza's theory of the emotions is quite consonant with what our best neuro-science is telling us about the affects.[9]

Another source of interest in Spinoza today is the environmental movement. Although Spinoza was himself no environmentalist, he had a strong conception of the unity and divinity of nature along with an acute sense of our utter dependency on the natural environment. These aspects of his thought have evoked an interest on the part of a number of environmentalists, especially those of the so-called 'deep-ecology' movement.

Another source of interest in Spinoza's philosophy is what some see as a similarity to the views of certain Asian religious and philosophical systems. As early as 1697, in Bayle's *Dictionnaire* article, scholars noticed a kind of doctrinal affinity. The view of nature as all-encompassing, unitary, timeless and purposeless has reminded some readers of Taoism. Some have seen in Spinoza's monism a reflection of Sankaracharya's *advaita* doctrine. Some have found in the cognitive therapy for the passions a path to selfless Buddhist non-attachment.[10] One does not have to be a believer in the timeless ubiquity of the 'perennial philosophy' to find these parallels interesting.

NOW

Many people today are sceptical – or at least uncertain – about the claims of traditional 'revealed religion'. Modern secularists are not likely to believe in miracles, do not explain things in terms of God's will and are inclined to think that the universe, on the whole, is morally indifferent to us. It seems that if the scientists (and neuroscientists) are right, all macro-events in our world (including human actions) are determined to be as they are by the laws of nature. This would suggest that free will is an illusion. Our minds seem to be inseparable from our bodies and this would seem to suggest that there is no personal immortality. These are elements in the world view of many modern secular philosophers and lay-people. They are also central doctrines in Spinoza's world-view.

Spinoza does not find in this view grounds for despair. On the contrary, our world, understood in this way, affords him an opportunity to achieve freedom, peace and joy by living in a reasonable way, by understanding and loving nature, and by understanding himself and his emotions as parts of nature. A number of people today would like to think that a rational, scientific understanding of ourselves can yield freedom, peace and joy. But many fear that the opposite might be the case. Spinoza claims to have compelling logical arguments in favour of his more optimistic view. Much of the current interest in Spinoza, I believe, can be traced to the hope that we can learn something from him about how to find peace and meaning in a world that turns out to be very much as he described it over three centuries ago.

In the 330 years since his death there has never been as much active research and study of Spinoza as there is today. Though no wise person would claim to be completely confident in his or her interpretation of every proposition of the *Ethics*, we have, I think, a better understanding of the work than any generation of readers has ever had. We also have (especially since the publication of Israel's *Radical Enlightenment*) a better understanding of the widespread influence of the *Ethics* upon the European intellectual developments that have produced the world-view that we call modernity.

NOTES

1. Jonathan Israel, *Radical Enlightenment*. Oxford: Oxford University Press 2001, p. vi.
2. In a famous letter to Wedderkopf from 1671, for example, Leibniz seems to embrace a full-fledged necessitarianism. He later rejected this view, of course, but he recognized that his account of creation came dangerously close to entailing that conclusion.
3. A very readable recent account of the relationship between Leibniz and Spinoza can be found in Matthew Stewart, *The Courtier and the Heretic: Leibniz, Spinoza, and the Fate of God in the Modern World*. New York: W. W. Norton, 2006.
4. The earlier work was the anonymously published 'Penseés diverses sur la comète'.
5. This point is discussed by Moreau on p. 413 of his contribution to the *Cambridge Companion to Spinoza*.
6. The quote from Voltaire is mentioned in Frederick Pollock, *Spinoza: His Life and Philosophy*. London: Duckworth 1899, p. 363. A very good source on Boulainvilliers (from which I have taken most of the preceding discussion) is Chapter 30 of Israel, *Radical Enlightenment*, pp. 565–744.

7. See Israel's discussion in *Radical Enlightenment*, p. 657.
8. These houses, located in Rijnsburg and in The Hague, are still maintained today by the organization 'Vereniging het Spinozahuis'.
9. Antonio Damasio, *Looking for Spinoza*. Orlando: Harcourt, 2003.
10. The most fully developed of these arguments would be Jan Wetlesen, *The Sage and the Way: Spinoza's Ethics of Freedom*. Assen: Van Gorcum, 1979.

NOTES FOR FURTHER READING

TRANSLATIONS

In recent decades three good new translations of the *Ethics* into English have appeared. E. M. Curley, Samuel Shirley and G. H. R. Parkinson have all produced careful, readable and reliable texts. For serious study, the Curley text in volume 1 of the *Collected Works* is probably best because of the extensive and very helpful glossary/index for Latin and English. The other two, however, are also quite good and can be confidently recommended. The quotations in this *Reader's Guide* have come mostly from Curley, though occasionally from Shirley.

> Curley, E. M. (ed. and trans.), *The Collected Works of Spinoza, Vol. 1*. Princeton: Princeton University Press, 1985.
> This translation is also available in, *A Spinoza Reader*. Princeton: Princeton University Press, 1994.
> Parkinson, G. H. R. (trans.), *Ethics*. Oxford: Oxford University Press, 2000.
> Shirley, Samuel (trans.), *Ethics, Treatise on the Emendation of the Intellect and Selected Letters*. Indianapolis: Hackett Publishing Company, 1992.

SECONDARY LITERATURE

Book-length introductory studies
There are a number of book-length introductions to Spinoza's philosophy that focus primarily on the *Ethics*. The following are quite good.

> Allison, Henry E., *Benedictus de Spinoza: an Introduction*. New Haven: Yale University Press, 1987.
> Hampshire, Stuart, *Spinoza*. New York: Penguin Books, 1951.
> Lloyd, Genevieve, *Routledge Philosophy Guide Book to Spinoza and 'The Ethics'*. London: Routledge, 1996.

Nadler, Steven, *Spinoza's 'Ethics': an Introduction*. Cambridge: Cambridge University Press, 2006.

Pollock, Frederick, *Spinoza: His Life and Philosophy*. London: Duckworth, 1899.

Book-length studies and critical commentaries

The following works, focused primarily on the *Ethics*, provide more indepth analysis, argument and critical commentary. They are intended for the more advanced student of the text.

Bennett, Jonathan, *A Study of Spinoza's 'Ethics'*. Indianapolis: Hackett, 1986.

Hallett, H. F., *Benedictus de Spinoza: the Elements of his Philosophy*. London: Athlone Press, 1957.

Joachim, Harold H., *A Study of the Ethics of Spinoza*. Oxford: Clarendon Press, 1901.

Wetlesen, Jan, *The Sage and the Way: Spinoza's Ethics of Freedom*. Assen: Van Gorcum, 1979.

Wolfson, Harry Austryn *The Philosophy of Spinoza*. Cambridge, MA: Harvard University Press, 1934.

Studies of specialized topics

The following works address narrower and more specialized topics. They are arranged in the order in which these topics are discussed in this text.

Spinoza's life

Klever, W. N. A., 'Spinoza's life and works', in Don Garrett (ed.), *Cambridge Companion to Spinoza*. Cambridge: Cambridge University Press, 1996, pp. 13–60.

Nadler, Steven, *Spinoza: A Life*. Cambridge: Cambridge University Press, 1999.

Geometrical method

Curley, E. M., 'Spinoza's Geometric Method', *Studia Spinozana* 2, 1986, 151–69.

Garrett, Aaron, *Meaning in Spinoza's Method*. Cambridge: Cambridge University Press, 2003.

The structure of the metaphysics

Curley, E. M., *Spinoza's Metaphysics: An Essay in Interpretation*. Cambridge, MA: Cambridge University Press, 1969.

Friedman, Joel I., 'How the finite follows from the infinite in Spinoza's metaphysical system', *Synthese*, 69, (1986), 371–407.

NOTES FOR FURTHER READING

Determinism
Garrett, Don, 'Spinoza's necessitarianism', in Y. Yovel (ed.), *God and Nature: Spinoza's Metaphysics*. Leiden: Brill, 1991, pp. 191–218.

Theory of mind/mind–body problem
Della Rocca, Michael, *Representation and the Mind-Body Problem in Spinoza*. New York: Oxford University Press, 1996.

Matson, Wallace, 'Spinoza's Theory of Mind', *Monist* 55, (1971), 567–78.

Physics/theory of individuation
Jonas, Hans, 'Spinoza and the Theory of Organism', in Marjorie Grene (ed.), *Spinoza: A Collection of Critical Essays*. Garden City, NY: Doubleday/Anchor Press, (1973), pp. 259–78.

Lachterman, David R., 'The Physics of Spinoza's Ethics', in R. Shahan and J. Biro (eds), *Spinoza: New Perspectives*. Norman: University of Oklahoma Press, 1978, pp. 77–111.

Imaginatio
Bennett, Jonathan, 'Spinoza on Error', *Philosophical Papers* 15, 1986, 59–73.

De Deugd, C. D., *The Significance of Spinoza's First Kind of Knowledge*. Assen: Van Gorcum.

Wilson, Margaret D., 'Spinoza's Theory of Knowledge', in D. Garrett (ed.), *Cambridge Companion to Spinoza*. Cambridge: Cambridge University Press, 1996, pp. 89–141.

Theory of the emotions
Giancotti, Emilia, 'The Theory of the Affects in the Strategy of Spinoza's Ethics', in Y. Yovel (ed.), *Desire and Affect: Spinoza as Psychologist*. New York: Little Room Press, 1999, pp. 129–38.

Neu, Jerome, *Emotion, Thought and Therapy*. Berkeley: University of California Press, 1977.

Ethical theory
Curley, E. M., 'Spinoza's Moral Philosophy', in Marjorie Grene (ed.), *Spinoza: A Collection of Critical Essays*. Garden City, NY: Doubleday/Anchor Press, 1973, pp. 354–76.

Garrett, Don, 'A free man always acts honestly, not deceptively': freedom and the good in Spinoza's Ethics', in E. Curley and P. F. Moreau (eds), *Spinoza: Issues and Directions*. Leiden: Brill, 1990, 221–38.

Stoic influence
James, Susan, 'Spinoza the Stoic', in T. Sorrell (ed.), *The Rise of Modern Philosophy*. Oxford: Oxford University Press, 1993, pp. 289–316.

Rational therapy for the passions
Cook, J. Thomas, 'Self-Knowledge as Self-Preservation', in M. Grene and D. Nails (eds), *Spinoza and the Sciences*. Boston Studies in the Philosophy of Science, vol. 91. Dordrecht: Reidel, 1986.

Doctrine of freedom
Hampshire, Stuart, 'Spinoza and the Idea of Freedom', in P. Kashap (ed.), *Studies in Spinoza*. Berkeley: University of California Press, 1972, pp. 310–31.

Eternity of the mind
Schnepf, Robert, 'Wer oder was ist unsterblich (wenn überhaupt) Spinozas Theorie des ewigen Teils des endlichen Geistes', *Archiv für Geschichte der Philosophie*, 88, #2, (2006), 189–215.

Steinberg, Diane, 'Spinoza's Theory of the Eternity of the Mind', *Canadian Journal of Philosophy*, 11, (1981), 35–68.

Reception and influence
Damasio, Antonio, *Looking for Spinoza*. Orlando: Harcourt, 2003.

Israel, Jonathan, *Radical Enlightenment*. Oxford: Oxford University Press, 2001.

Moreau, Pierre-François, 'Spinoza's reception and influence', in D. Garrett (ed.), *Cambridge Companion to Spinoza*. Cambridge: Cambridge University Press, 1996, pp. 408–33.

INDEX

act
  defined via adequate cause 90, 116
  related to *conatus* 98
adequate cause 90, 116
adequate cognition
  and common notions 77
  of God's essence 79
  of passions 129
  requiring knowledge of causes 70–1
advaita 160
affects *see* emotions
akrasia
  defined and explained 111
  preventing action 112
amnesia, Spanish poet with 121–2
Amsterdam 3
animata 57
appetite 99
arete 114
Asian philosophy and religion 160
association, as explanation of language and memory 66
atheism
  charge of 1, 152
  Spinozism as 11, 152, 155
  the 'virtuous atheist' 154
attributes
  as conceptually ultimate 25
  definition 25
  as essence of substance 25
  extension as 25
  infinite number of 26, 27, 55
  no causal interaction between 49, 53, 91
  subjective interpretation of 27
  thought as 25
  thought as related to extension (parallelism) 47, 50

Bayle, Pierre
  on Asian overtones in Spinoza 160
  Dictionnaire historique et critique 154
  on the 'virtuous atheist' 154
beings of the imagination (*entia imaginationis*)
  differences in perception among individuals 46
  explanation of 45
  faculties of intellect and will 85–6
  good, evil, beauty, ugliness 45
blessedness (*beatitudo*) 14, 16, 120, 127
bodies, simplest and composite 58
Boulainvilliers, Henri, Comte de 155
British Hegelians 158

INDEX

causal determinism
  definition/explanation 11, 39–40
  Descartes rejects 12
  and free will 12
  in human body and mind 85
  and moral responsibility 12
  and rejection of miracles 11
  universal 20, 53
causation
  adequate 90, 116
  billiard ball example 38–9
  immanent and transient 34–5
  none between attributes 49, 52, 91
  related to logical implication 20
  universal 20, 53
  vertical and horizontal orders of 39, 52
Christian morality, compared with Spinoza's ethics 123–4
cognition, adequate *see* adequate cognition
cognitive therapy for the passions
  'dilution' of passion via understanding of causes 133
  via adequate understanding of the passions 128–32
  via recognition of necessity 133–5
Coleridge, Samuel Taylor 158
common notions (*notiones communes*)
  always adequate 77
  defined and explained 77–8
  extension and motion as examples of 78
  geometry and laws of nature 78–9
  present in every mind 145
composite bodies
  human body as 60
  individuation of 58–60, 95
  ratio of motion and rest definitive of 58, 95
  theory of organism 59

conatus
  and desire 99
  explained 93–7
  as force or power 98
  and inertia 94, 96
  as primary basis of virtue 115
conceptual dependence 21
contentment of mind (*acquiescentia animi*) 147
Copernicus 6
Curley, E. M. 37

Damasio, Antonio 160, 162n. 9
Democritus 8
dependence, conceptual and ontological 21
Descartes, René
  on deduction and intuition 139
  on free will in action 12, 47, 68
  on free will in belief formation 86
  on God's creation of logic 33, 41
  mind–body dualism 13, 26, 47
  mind–body interaction 48
  and the 'new natural philosophy' 6, 8–9, 13
  pineal gland role 48, 128
  on primary and secondary qualities 46
  problem of error 68
  René Descartes' The Principles of Philosophy demonstrated in the geometric manner (Spinoza) 9, 18
  on skepticism and doubt 82
desire 99
determinism *see* causal determinism
divine nature, all things following from 31

ecology (deep ecology) 160
egoism 114

INDEX

emotions
  active and passive 103
  to be explained naturalistically 89
  factors affecting strength of 112–13
  passive *see* passions
  Spinoza's focus on 88
  three basic 98–100
  in traditional ethical theory 14
endeavor *see* conatus
Enden, Franciscus van den 4, 9
Enlightenment 152, 155
Epictetus 134
error
  as a central problem 68–9
  in emotions 101
  'nothing positive' 76
  resulting from incompleteness 69–71
essence
  attributes as God's essence 25
  of body under form of eternity 143–4
  conatus as 140–1
  formal, of non-existent things 51
  God's essence as infinite power 31, 140
  individual, contained (eternally) in the attributes 51, 141
eternity
  of mathematical truths 142
  of mind without memory or imagination 144
  reason knows things as 'under a certain form of' (*sub quadam specie aeternitatis*) 83, 142
  timelessness of infinite modes 35
Ethics
  five-part structure 16
  Part 2 (outline) 47
  Part 4 (outline) 104–5, 126–7
  Part 5 (outline) 129
  translations of 151, 155, 156

Euclid 17
expulsion from Jewish community (Spinoza) 1, 4
extension
  as an attribute of substance 25
  of God 30

falsity
  consisting in privation 75
  as 'nothing positive' 75–6
fear of death 148
first kind of knowledge *see* imagination (imaginatio)
Frederick the Great 156
'free man', characteristics of 125
free will
  defined/explained 84
  Descartes embraces 12
  erroneous belief in 75
  and error in Descartes 68
  God without free will 34, 41
  and purposive (teleological) explanation 43
  role in belief (for Descartes) 86
  Spinoza denies 12, 105
  Spinoza's argument against 41, 84–7
  thrown-stone analogy 85
freedom
  choice not part of 33
  conceptually tied to activity and power 106
  definition 32
  God as only free cause 32
  the way to 127
Freud, Sigmund 159

Galilei, Galileo
  on math as language of nature 17
  and the new 'natural philosophy' 6, 17
  on primary and secondary qualities 46

INDEX

geometrical method
  Euclid's *Elements* as model 17
  model of clarity and certainty 18
  reasons for Spinoza's use of 17–19
God
  as all-encompassing 10, 29, 42
  an extended being 31
  cannot be hated 133
  first cause 10, 29
  'God of the philosophers' 28
  having no emotions 137
  having no free will 33, 41, 43
  how 'acts' 32
  identified with substance 19
  as 'immanent cause' of all 34–5
  love of 14, 136, 137, 147–8
  mind of 51, 54
  necessary existence of 26, 42
  as only free cause 32, 42
  rejection of traditional 9, 10, 28, 34, 42, 137
  Spinoza's use of the term 28
  as subject of *Ethics,* Part 1 19
Goethe, Johann Wolfgang von 157–8
good
  defined with reference to model of human nature 108–9
  as joy and sadness 102–3
  'nothing positive in things' 108

hatred 100
Hegel, Georg Wilhelm Friedrich 158
Hegelians, British 158
Heidelberg professorship offer 5
Hobbes, Thomas, influence on Spinoza's political views 8, 119–21
human nature, model of 108–9
humility 102, 123

ideas
  human mind as idea of body 54–6
  of ideas 67
  involving affirmation 86
  modally identical with its *ideatum* 51
  as modes under attribute of thought 49
  in same order and connection as things (parallelism) 49–50
  of things 49–51
  two, of Peter 65
imagination (*imaginatio*)
  confused and mutilated 73
  first kind of knowledge 80
  not erroneous per se 65
  perception as 64–5
  as source of inadequacy 73
  see also beings of the imagination (*entia imaginationis*)
immanent cause 34–5
inadequate cognition
  belief in free will as example of 75
  of the body 71
  defined and explained 70
  of the duration of things 73
  effect on emotions 101
  of external things 73
  lacking ideas of causes 70–1
  of the mind 72
inertia
  and *conatus* 94, 96
  in Spinoza's physics 58
infinite and eternal modes
  Curley's interpretation of 36–7
  immediate 35–6
  mediate 37
intellectual love of God (*amor Dei intellectualis*) 147–8
intuitive knowledge (*intuitio*)
  defined 81, 139
  in Descartes 139
  explained 140

INDEX

how it differs from reason 139
intuitive self-knowledge 146–7
third kind of knowledge 81
Israel, Jonathan 7n. 2, 152

Jacobi, F. H. 157
jealousy 102
Jewish community, Spinoza's
    expulsion from 1, 4
Joachim, Harold H. 71
Jonas, Hans 59
joy (*laetitia*)
    increase in power to act 100
    knowledge of goodness 112
    one of three basic emotions 100
    striving for 100
    translation as 'pleasure' 150n. 12
    value of simple joys 122

Kant, Immanuel 126
knowledge
    of God
        the mind's greatest good 116, 119
        yields love of God 136
    of good and evil 112
    types of *see* imagination
        (*imaginatio*); intuitive
        knowledge (*intuitio*); reason
        (*ratio*)

language 66
laws of nature
    'containing' formal essences of
        non-existent things 52
    and infinite and eternal modes 36–7
Leeuwenhoek, Antony von 3
Leibniz, Wilhelm Gottfried von
    doctrine of possible worlds 41–2
    in touch with and influenced by
        Spinoza 153
Lessing, Gotthold Ephraim 157

love
    defined 100
    derived from joy 100
    of enemies 123
    of God 136, 137, 147–8
Lucretius 8

Maimonides, Moses 8
memory 66
Mendelssohn, Moses 157
Meyer, Lodewijk 18
mind
    contentment of (*acquiescentia animi*) 147
    differing as bodies differ 57
    of God
        all modes under attribute of thought 51
        human mind a part of 54
    human, as idea of body 54–5
    as nothing but ideas 56
mind–body dualism
    Descartes embraces 13, 26, 47–8
    Spinoza rejects 13, 26, 48
miracles
    explanation of 45
    rejection of 11, 45
model of human nature
    used to define 'good' and 'bad' 108–9
    see also 'free man', characteristics of
modes
    entirely dependent on and determined by God 37
    finite, following from God 38–9
    'in' substance 30
    modus as 'way' 30
    physical things as 30
    see also infinite and eternal modes
motion and rest, ratio of, to define composite bodies 58, 95

INDEX

natura naturans and *natura naturata* 40, 82
natural laws *see* laws of nature
natural right 119
nature
  divine, all things following from 31
  human, model of 108–9
necessity
  of all things 31, 39
  of God's nature as it is 32
  reason knowing all things as necessary 83
  recognition reducing passions 133
neuroscience 160
Nietzsche, Friedrich 159
Novalis (Friedrich von Hardenberg) 158

ontological dependence 21
Opera Posthuma see Posthumous Works
Ovid on akrasia 111

pantheism
  'Pantheismusstreit' dispute 157
  term coined by Toland 154
parallelism
  derived from substance-attribute metaphysics 49–50
  problem of non-existent modes 51
  role in theory of perception 62
passions
  adequate cognition of 129
  caused from without 110
  engendering excessive desires 124
  forming a clear and distinct idea of 131
  humans always subject to 110
  as motives to good actions 124
  as source of disagreements 118

passivity
  as conceptually tied to servitude 106
  see also passions
perception
  confusion inherent in 63
  general theory of 62
  mechanics of 64
  of mind concerning body 55
perfection 107
personal identity criteria 121
philosophy of mind (current) 159
physics
  principle of inertia 58
  of simplest and composite bodies 58
  in Spinoza's writings 58–61
poet, Spanish, with amnesia 121–2
Posthumous Works
  in Jefferson's library 155
  surreptitious publication and ban of 2, 5–6, 151
  translated into Dutch 151
power
  to act 99
  and freedom 106
  God/substance as 30
  identical with virtue 114
  increase and diminution of 99
primary and secondary qualities 46
proportionals 81
purposes
  explanation by reference to 43
  God as purposeless 44
  purposive (teleological) explanation 43

ratio of motion and rest, as defining composite bodies 58, 95
rationalist, Spinoza as 18
reason (*ratio*)
  leading to agreement 118
  as motive for action 124

INDEX

necessarily active 115
not engendering excessive desire 124
as second kind of knowledge 81
Reformation 6
religion, Spinoza's critique of 1, 10
Rembrandt van Rijn 3
Renaissance
  awareness of classical culture 6
  interest in mathematics 17
repentance 123
revealed religion, Spinoza's critique of 1, 10
Rousseau's *Emile* 155
Royal Academy of Sciences (Berlin) 156
Russell, Bertrand 159

sadness (*tristitia*)
  as decrease in power to act 100
  as knowledge of evil 112
  one of three basic emotions 100
  sometimes translated as 'pain' 150n. 12
  striving to avoid 100
salvation 16
Santayana, George 159
Schadenfreude 102
Schmidt, Johann Lorenz 156
second kind of knowledge *see* reason (*ratio*)
sense-perception *see* perception
servitude, and passivity/passions 106
simplest bodies 58
social contract 120
Socrates, on weak will 111
Soviet Union, Spinoza reception in 159
Spanish poet with amnesia 121–2
Spinoza reception in Soviet Union 159
Spinoza Societies today 159

state of nature
  in Hobbes and Spinoza 119–21
  no right or wi in 120
state (theory of) 119–21
Stoics
  controlling emotions via will 128
  desiring what is necessary 126
  influence on Spinoza's ethics 8
  recognition of limits of our power 134
  on self-preservation 93
  on virtue 114
  see also Epictetus
Studia Spinozana 159
substance
  causa sui (cause of itelf) 23, 24
  Descartes' definition of 21
  as identical with God 26
  indivisible 28–9
  infinite 24
  requiring no explanation 21
  singular 23, 24
  Spinoza's definition of 21
suicides, and *conatus* doctrine 97–8
sun (our perception of) 75–6, 110–11, 130

Taoism 160
teleological (purposive) explanation 43
Theological-Political Treatise
  composition of 5
  influence on *Wertheim Bible* 156
  in Jefferson's library 155
  political theory of 119
  publication and prohibition of 1
  translations of 154
third kind of knowledge *see* intuitive knowledge (*intuitio*)
titillation (*titillatio*) 122
Toland, John 10, 154

INDEX

Tractatus Theologico-politicus see Theological-Political Treatise
transient cause 34–5
translation of *Ethics*
  into French by Boulainvilliers (unpublished) 155
  into German by Schmidt 156
  as part of *Opera Posthuma* 151
Treatise on the Emendation of the Intellect 15
triangles, examples of necessity 32, 33, 42
Tschirnhaus, Ehrenfried Walther von 35

understanding
  highest good 116
  known to be certain good 115
  pleasurable activity 116
universals 79–80, 85–6

vacillation 101
virtue
  as its own reward 148
  as power 114
  as understood by Greeks 114
'virtuous atheist' 154
Vries, Simon de 5

weak will *see* akrasia
Wertheim Bible 156
will
  and *conatus* 99
  consisting of individual volitions 41
  God's having none 34, 40
  'God's will' as the sanctuary of ignorance 44
  volitions as determined modes of thought 84
  weak *see* akrasia
  see also free will
Wolff, Christian 155–6
Wordsworth, William 158

zero-sum goods 119